The Spiritual Writings Of Annie Rix Militz

by

Annie Rix Militz

PART I.

LESSON I. FIRST PRINCIPLES.

AS with our mental eyes we look forth over the world and consider its people, and what they are living for, and what they are most earnestly desiring, we find that all mankind have one common pursuit, and all are desirous of but one thing, and that is Happiness.

No matter by what name they are calling their desire, whether it is power, honors, riches, health, peace, love, or knowledge, everyone and all can be summed up and brought under the one name, Happiness.

Not only does everyone pursue happiness, but everyone at sometime believes that he can have it, and at all times he believes that he has a right to have it.

Some think that they have ceased to look for happiness - the word seems too large to them, but there is one word that represents what they think they can have here and now, and that word is Satisfaction.

"Oh, to be satisfied!" they cry, "Oh, to be at rest!" Yes, it is true all can have satisfaction, and not only may we be passively, quietly satisfied, but it is our right and our privilege to be happy actively, joyously happy here and now, with not a sorrow to mar our joy, not one thing that can interfere with our happiness. In other words, we can enter into eternal, unchanging bliss now, in this time, and it is right for us to believe so to believe that all good is for us to-day, and to ask, to seek, to knock until we are consciously one with our own true state of being, pure happiness.

All along the ages have arisen great souls, grand masters of life, who have believed in man's right to happiness, and, believing so, have given all they had, their whole lives, all their energy, love, and whatever they prized into the service of finding how this happiness may be attained, and, with one accord, we find of them saying that to know the Truth and to live the Truth is the one and the only Way to eternal happiness, and he who once knows the whole Truth, need never know sickness, sorrow, evil, death, poverty, or any other wretchedness ever again.

"Ye shall know the truth, and the truth shall make you free." -John 8:32. Free from what? Free from every evil condition; free from every material limitation to which mortals seem so in bondage. And if we are not free, if something still prevents us from having what we desire or doing that which we wish to do, then we may know that we must rise up out of some ignorance, and we must seek and receive the whole Truth, for it must be the whole Truth that shall set us wholly free.

It has been argued that when we have found the whole Truth we shall know it, in that it fulfills three conditions of perfect happiness. It should give us (1) Health of body, (2) Peace of mind, (3) The key to all knowledge. Since these three conditions have been fulfilled in students by these teachings we see that we can truly call this gospel, Truth.

In order that we may walk the Way with understanding and profit we must, in this first lesson, see that we start from the same point that is, that we all stand together upon one Foundation Principle, and standing together there, we shall see that we cannot but walk together from principle to principle, and every deduction and conclusion must be taken from alpha to omega. We shall know that if we have not believed in all these principles, and not only believed them but lived them, that it will not be hard for us to understand why we have not had that happiness we desire, or manifested that perfection we would show forth.

The first principle of Truth is: God is good and God is omnipresent. Upon the acceptance of this principle depends your receptivity to all that follows.

"Come now, let us reason together, saith the Lord." Is. 1 :18. There are three statements in the wording of this principle which may be called the first axioms of Truth, viz:

1 God is.

2 God is the Good.

3 God is omnipresent.

An axiom is defined as a self-evident truth. Taking this definition in its highest sense we can see why the truth "God is" can be called axiomatic. No external evidence or human argument can prove to you that God is. Such can be corroborative witness to what you have already received from within, but let us rest forever in this understanding that only God can prove to you that God is, and that proof comes from the divine within yourself.

Every thinker believes in a cause back of all that he observes about him. Some call this great cause Force, some, Nature, some, Law, some, The Great First Cause, some, The Unknowable, but by far the greater part of those who have most earnestly pondered upon the idea have given it the name of some deity. In these teachings we have chosen to use the name God, because it includes all that is in the other names and more. The name Force would seem to exclude the attribute of love, Nature seems often strangely blind and merciless, while with the name God it is not difficult with most people to associate those higher qualities omitted from the others. Another advantage accruing to the name God is that it is one in its Anglo-Saxon root with the word Good.

Let us now consider our second axiom, "God is the Good."

It is agreed by all the wise that have most blessed the world that the First Cause is good. Those who call it Force, or Law, agree that it is good, as evidenced in the theory of "the survival of the fittest," or best, in all species. The devotee of Nature believes that all her efforts are towards bringing forth health, beauty, and good in manifold ways. It is not difficult for us to agree that God is good. Let us enlarge upon this basic statement, God is the Good. What do we mean by the Good?

The highest goodness must be that which is so good that it is never anything else. It is that which is everlastingly, unchangeably, universally good in other words, the Absolute Good.

God is that Good which is good for all people at all times and in all places. It is not that which is good for one race and not for another, or for one sex and not for another, or for one age and not for another ; that is only relative goodness, passing shadows finally swallowed up by that sun of righteousness the Great Good of All.

If we begin to consider that which everyone believes is good for himself we shall enter upon infinity, for the good things of God cannot be numbered. We will state a few in order to lay our foundation stones :

1 HEALTH is GOOD. Everyone believes that health is good for himself and good for his loved one. Always, everywhere, health is good. Listen to this simple logic, this syllogism:

Since God is Good,
And Health is Good,
Therefore God is Health
And Health is God.

"For I shall yet praise him, who is the health of my countenance, and my God." Ps. 42:11.

2 LIFE is GOOD. By Life is not meant that condition of earthly affairs between birth and death not many see that good but that Principle, that Power that lies back of the sparkle in the eye and the glow on the cheek, that great Essence and Presence whose beginnings materialists have, all in vain, so ardently sought. No mortal has ever touched Life or confined It to form or definition, but all agree that It is as unknowable and undefinable as God, and, like Deity, only appreciable through Its effects or manifestations.

Listen to our reasoning:

Since God is Good
And Life is Good,

Therefore God is Life
And Life is God.

3 SUBSTANCE is GOOD. What is Substance ? Metaphysicians define it as that which is the reality of being, that which is the genuine, indestructible presence that is back of the appearance called "matter." Its essence is unchangeability. It is eternal, incorruptible, infinite, and unlimited. It is Being, of which materiality is the shadow. What is Substance with the metaphysician is Spirit with the theologian, and in these teachings Substance and Spirit are synonymous terms used interchangeably.

Again we reason:

Since God is Good,
And Substance is Good,
Therefore God is Substance
And Substance is God.

"God is Spirit," says Jesus (Wilson's Emphatic Diaglot). God is one Spirit, in, and through, and the reality of all manifestation the beauty, grandeur, and glory of the universe.

By this time the observing student will be cognizant of our methods of meditation and deduction, and can himself start with correct premises and arrive at true conclusions, proving to his own satisfaction that God is all that is pure Goodness universally, eternally,, impartially good.

Practice meditating upon what is good for all people at all times and in all places, and then see how God is that, and your foundation is sure.

4 LOVE is GOOD. Unselfish, pure, unchangeable Love is good for all. God is Love.

5 INTELLIGENCE is GOOD. God is Intelligence -- Wisdom.

6 TRUTH is GOOD. God is Truth.

We need not put any limit to our enumeration of the Goodness that is God. God is Peace, Prosperity, Purity, Strength, Trust, Faith, Rest, Power, Freedom, and so on to infinity. But it is enough for our foundation Statement of Being to dwell upon certain thoughts of God now, and charge our minds with one short statement only: God is Health, Life, Love, Truth, Substance, and Intelligence.

Let us now consider our third axiom, "God is Omnipresent."

God is everywhere. God fills all, and is the very being of all that is. God is All in All. Let us see to what conclusions the acknowledgment that God is omnipresent will lead us. Since God is good and God is omnipresent, then Good is omnipresent, Good is everywhere. Since God is Health and God is omnipresent, health is omnipresent, health is in and through all things. Life is omnipresent, love is omnipresent, truth is omnipresent, substance is omnipresent, intelligence is omnipresent.

All that can be predicated of God can be declared true of all that is good. God is Omnipotence, therefore health is omnipotent, and so also is life and love.

Repetition of these truths in every conceivable form is the mental method of hammering, "driving home,' 7 stamping, and solidifying the foundation of that building which is to be the center and headquarters of all our coming demonstrations. Too much attention cannot be paid to this first lesson. A student that is well grounded upon the basic principles will find all the subsequent lessons easy to comprehend and practice.

Who are you? "Know thyself has ever been the inspired injunction. Every sage has expressed this thought in some manner: "If man would only study himself and know himself, then he would know all things nothing would be unknown to him." This is true. If man knows the true Self of him, then he must know God, for the true Self is one with God.

Moses spoke of Man's oneness with God as Man being made in the image and likeness of God. Jesus spoke of Man's oneness with God as the Son being one with the Father. "I and the Father are one."

God is divine Mind. Man is its Idea. God creates or thinks Man. God thinks upon Himself, images Himself, speaks the word, "I am." Man is that Word.

You are the thought of God, the idea of the divine Mind. You have no existence apart from God. The perfect Mind never loses one of its thoughts ; so you, God's thought, cannot be lost out of His mind. "In him we live, and move, and have our being."

The thought is always like the thinker, therefore Scripture says Man, who is the thought, is like God, who is the thinker.

Therefore this is the truth which you must speak for yourself and realize is true : Since God is Health, I, who am the image of God, must be healthy not sick. It is true that I am, in reality, strong and well.

Since God is Spirit, I am Spirit. I am, in reality, spiritual, immortal, healthy, and harmonious.

I am Divine, not mortal;

I am Holy, not sinful;

I am Wise, not ignorant,

Because God is All,

And beside Him there is none else.

The Idea of God is one with God. Since God is All in the universe, there is only God only God and His Idea, His Son, and that Idea is God. For since God is All, there is only God for God to think upon. "This is life eternal, that they might know thee, the only true God [the Father] and Jesus Christ [Man, the Son] whom thou hast sent."

The real Self of you is the Christ, one with the Father. You are not a mortal, sickly, weak, and foolish being, as it would seem you are. In reality you are all that is everlastingly divine and perfect. This is the truth about yourself.

It is not enough to listen to these teachings only, they must be practiced. These truths must be used in order that they may be proven good and desirable. We know that with music, one will not be proficient who only listens to the theories, but does not apply them. So it is with the Life. We must live its principles every day every hour, every moment thinking some good thought, some God-thought.

If one hears, that is, listens carefully and obediently to these lessons, and then practices them all he can, he has built his house upon a rock, and no matter how he may be assailed by sickness or trouble, it can get no hold upon him, but he will stand, and the more the storm beats about his house the more secure he will feel himself within.

But he that hears, be he ever so attentive and pleased with the doctrine, but does not do may know why some problems seem too hard for him, and sickness and disaster undermine him.

Build upon rock by continual practice of the Word. Jesus called this "praying always."

In the interim between the study of a lesson and the next hold this statement in mind, often silently repeating it : Only the Good is true.

Copy the following, and mentally repeat it every night and morning :

God is Health, Life, Love, Truth, Substance, Intelligence.

God is All.

God is Omnipresence, Omnipotence, and Omniscience.

I am the Thought of God, the Idea of the divine Mind. In Him I live, move, and have my being. I am spiritual, harmonious, fearless, and free. I am governed by the law of God, the everlasting Good, and I am not subject to the law of sin, sickness, and death.

I know the Truth, and the Truth makes me free from evil in every form and from all material bondage, now and forever.

God works through me to will and to do whatever ought to be done by me.

I am happy. I am holy. I am loving. I am wise.

I and the Father are one. Amen.

LESSON II. THE REAL AND THE UNREAL.

HE first lesson the student of Truth must learn is summed up in the answer of Jesus Christ to the scribe who asked him what was the first commandment, or rule, for right living:

"And Jesus answered him, The first of all the commandments is, Hear, O Israel; The Lord our God is one Lord: And thou shalt love the Lord thy God with all thy heart, and with all thy soul, and with all thy mind and with all thy strength: this is the first commandment. And the second is like, namely this, Thou shalt love thy neighbor as thyself. " Mark 12:29-31.

God must be loved with the whole nature, and this is only possible as we know that God is all that really is. God is the One Good, everywhere present. God is the One Spirit, the One Mind in everybody. God is the One Substance in the universe. God is the One Life, Health, Love, Truth, Substance, and Intelligence.

God is the only Self in us and in our neighbor. Therefore the second commandment is just the same as the first, for if we love God with all our heart, soul, mind, and strength, what love have we left for ourselves or our neighbor unless the real Self in us be God?

There is only God. There is no reality in anything that is not God.

It is written, "Ye shall know the truth, and the truth shall make you free." This is true, and as we look about us and see the human race so in bondage to evil we have but one conclusion in our minds it must be that they do not know the Truth. Some seem free from one thing but are in bondage to another; others are almost entirely free, yet something still limits and binds, and in the case of these we must conclude that they have received but part of the Truth, or have been contented with a mixture of Truth and error, for when once they know the whole Truth, and practice it, they must be wholly free. Part-truths heal us only in part.

Why is it that men who are preaching what they believe to be the Truth are sick and poor, weak and full of sorrow and trouble?

This is the reason: While they declare God to be good and to be omnipotent, in the same breath they begin to talk of another power called evil, the devil, as very strong and powerful, which is continually warring against God, and most of the time prevailing.

At the same time that men have said God is omnipresent, everywhere present, they talk of another being, exactly opposite to God, the Good, as a real presence, and even ascribe to it the All-presence that belongs to God. Thus they break their first commandment : "Thou shalt have no other gods [powers] before me."

To give evil even the smallest presence is to put it in the place where God should be yes, where God really is. They should know the omnipresence of the Good only, and acknowledge that in order to be free from the evil in which they have so long been believing.

Gautama Buddha, the great Eastern sage, after days of prayer and fasting, desiring above all things to know why his people suffered so, received this word from the Divine Spirit : "The reason of suffering is ignorance. Teach the people the truth, and they shall be free." It is ignorance of God that we must rise out of in order to be set free from those ills that are the results of it. And this ignorance is expressed by the people as a belief in the universal presence of evil. From this error every mind must be set free by being imbued with the idea of the universal presence of God.

Is it reasonable to say that God is good and all-powerful, and then say that evil has any power at all ? Is it reasonable to believe in the omnipresence of God and at the same time think the devil has any real presence? Come, let God in you speak to you the whole Truth!

Since God is the Good and God is everywhere, Good must be everywhere, and there is no real presence to evil at all. Since God is all and He is the one creator, He must create all out of His own substance, which is Good. God creates Good only. "And God saw that it was good."

"And God saw everything that he had made, and, behold, it was very good." Gen. 1:31. Good is all that really is made. There is, in reality, no place for evil in God's universe. Evil has no real presence, or power, or law, and all that can be classed under the head of evils are delusions and unrealities, and should be recognized as only such.

Sin, sickness, sorrow, death, have no place in the omnipresence of God.

God does not think impure, unholy thoughts, therefore sinful desires, words, and deeds have no part or place in the true Self. There is no reality in sin; it is without power, law, or substance.

God is omnipresent Health. There is no pain, no sickness, no disease in God. There is nothing in God to be sick or out of which to make disease, therefore He does not make pain, sickness or disease. There is no reality in disease.

God is immortal, changeless Life, omnipresent Life. Life does not end. There is no reality in death. Absence of life is an appearance, and no one ever really dies. Death has no real place or power in God's world.

God is Spirit pure, holy, unlimited, eternal, perfect Substance. Since God is all, His creation must be in and of Himself, in and of His substance, therefore the world of God must be Spiritual and not material. Matter is not the real substance of the universe, for the qualities of matter change, decay, limitation, mortality, and imperfection have no place in divine manifestation. Materiality is negation.

All the beauty, grandeur, life, and goodness of creation are Spiritual, not material, and therefore they are eternal to the mind that truly knows and to the eyes that really see.

Not only must we believe in the omnipresence and omnipotence of God, but we must carry that belief to its ultimate extent, which is to believe that there can be no reality in any other presence or power. We cannot allow the claim of any presence other than Good and Spirit to take hold upon our minds in order to be loyal to the greatest command of all : 'Thou shalt love the Lord thy God with all thy mind." "In all thy ways acknowledge him." Prov. 3 :6. "Look unto me and be ye saved, all the ends of the earth : for I am God, and there is none else." Is. 45 :22.

The Greek philosopher Zeno says: "The most necessary part of learning is to unlearn our errors." The mind that comes up to the fountain of Truth to partake of its blessings must first be placed in a receptive condition, must first be cleansed of its belief in the reality of evil and materiality, in order that it may receive the full Truth, and this cleansing process is accomplished by the word of negation.

Every negative word erases, and to erase false thoughts from the mind the word of denial must be spoken.

In the first chapter of Genesis the mind that awaits the coming of Truth is spoken of in the language of symbolism as the earth, without form and void "and darkness was upon the face of the deep." Darkness is the symbol of ignorance, and light is the symbol of Truth. "And God said [to the waiting mind], Let there be light [Truth] : and there was light."

Denial makes us receptive. "And God said. Let there be" as though the earth must let the light shine. And so it is. The mind must let the Truth come in. "Prepare ye the way of the Lord, make his paths straight," by beginning to clear out the rubbish of false thinking pulling up the "plants which my Father hath not planted."

People who have sick bodies, or vices, or inharmonious surroundings are like pupils who have worked their problems incorrectly, and before they begin to work them aright they must first erase their old work, then begin the working anew with true principles for their bases of operations.

Right denial pulls down old, false structures built by vain imaginings, and leaves the mind ready to build anew.

Every religion has taught denial in some form. All fasting is but the symbol of the denying which is going on in mind. Sacrifices represent the putting away, or the denying of the power of "the world, the flesh, and the devil " Fanatics have cut and lacerated their bodies, and sat in sack, cloth and ashes, to signify their realization of the vanity or unreality of the earthly body and worldly life. In truth, the real denial was all the time in mind, and no external ceremony could make them realize the nothingness of the worldly life and ways if they were not trying in all sincerity to realize it in heart and mind. We see this proven by people going through long fasts and other external forms of denial, and yet not realizing any more spirituality after them than before. All real denial begins in the heart and mind.

The process of denial is represented in the Scriptures by John the Baptist, who, it was prophesied, must come first in order to prepare the way of the Lord, the full Gospel.

"Repent ye! Repent ye!" was John's cry. The literal translation of the Greek *metamoia* (mistranslated "repent ye") is "Change your mind." In other words, stop thinking about sin, and so stop the doing and speaking it. Change your mind as to what are the realities of life, and seek the things of the Spirit. "Except ye become converted [turned right about] and become as little children [who know no evil] ye cannot enter into the kingdom of heaven."

"If any man will come after me, let him deny himself." How is it that Jesus denied himself? By beginning in heart and mind to set aside the fleshly man. He says, "If I honor myself, my honor is nothing;" "I speak not of myself, it is the Father that dwelleth in me, he doeth the works." He denied his personality, for he knew that that was not the real Self. He knew Himself to be Spirit, not flesh. "The flesh profiteth nothing," he said. He knew himself to be Immortal, not mortal as he seemed to be. He said, "Judge not by the appearance, but judge righteous judgment." We, too, are Spiritual, not material; divine Immortals, not carnal and mortal. We deny the reality of the carnal mind and body under the name "personality." It is a good term to express all the collective errors that man has held about himself. The word "person" (from the Latin per and sona, to sound through) was originally applied to a mask which ancient actors wore upon the stage. Most personalities seem to hide the real nature of the individual beautiful natures obscured by ugly forms and features, great souls curtained by diminutive bodies. Denial of personality draws aside the curtain, dissolves the imperfect, and reveals the translucent body through which the Spirit shines and works untrammeled.

The fleshly body is not yourself, and nothing done to it can hurt you. Mentally look at all personality as you would look through darkness to the light. Deny its actions, its foolishness, its sickness, its weakness, its meanness, its wickedness, and these will melt before your true word like mist before the sun.

To remember to meet every evil claim, suggestion or appearance with the silent assertion, "There is no evil" is to be a light in the midst of darkness, causing the evil to fly and the real good that was there all the time to come forward in all its strength and power.

You are like one who continually says to false report, "That is not so," and it cannot influence you because you will not believe in it. All evil is a lie, a delusion, and it has power to those only who believe in it. Thus Jesus defines evil and its author : "He was a murderer from the beginning and abode not in the truth, because there is no truth in him. When he speaketh a lie, he speaketh of his own : for he is a liar and the father of it." No matter how true a statement may seem to be, if it is not true of God, then it must be known as a relative truth or a lie, and we are not to be deceived by it. One way to lift the mind from believing in evil is to look at the falsities squarely and fearlessly, and say: "You are not real, you are not true. It is nothing. It has no real and true creator, and I will not believe in it any longer." But the most terse, effective, even drastic, denial that one can speak is embodied in those words, "There is no evil."

If you believe the mirage on the desert is a reality, a real lake of waters surrounded by trees, then you will pursue it as long as you are deceived, and endure many sufferings and hardships through your ignorance. But the traveler who knows it to be nothing, says so, and cannot be deluded into following it nor led out of his way, no matter how fair it may be to look upon. So should we regard all evil and all this dream-world which passes away continually, and which all prophets have pronounced 'Vanity of vanities," and "its nations as nothing in the eyes of the Lord."

"But can I not believe my senses ?" the mortal cries. Surely not, since the senses are continually contradicting each other, as has been proven both by experiments and natural experiences. Even material science contradicts the senses. For example, the sun seems to rise and set, but astronomy tells us that that is but an appearance, and it is the earth that moves and not the sun. The senses say the moon is a flat disc, astronomy declares it to be a sphere ; the stars seem points of light, whereas it is said that some are suns many thousand times greater than our sun.

We are not now looking to our senses for Truth, but to the divine Reason within us, and to our Intuition, "that light which lighteth every man that cometh into the world."

When thy senses affirm that which thy reason denies, reject the testimony of thy senses, and listen only to thy reason. Maimonides.

The mind that is determined to believe in God alone faithfully takes up the denial of all that is not God, and, as he walks along the Way, he soon begins to see that Truth proves itself true. What of is the result of persistently holding, right in the face of appearances, to the thought, "There is no reality to sin; no real power, presence, or law to sin?"

It is to see vice and impure thinking drop right out of your own mind and life, and not only yours, but out of those for whom you speak the words. Does the denial of the reality of sin cause license, making people more sinful and wicked? Not at all. On the contrary it causes them to see that there is no pleasure in it, that there is no satisfaction in it, and a great realization of the uselessness and powerlessness of sin comes to the faithful student. For the saying is true, and Truth, boldly spoken though in silence, is a living power in itself capable of freeing from every bondage even of sin itself.

When the mind that dwells in the consciousness of God sends forth its word denying any place or power to sickness, pain, disease, then we see health spring forth as flowers spring up when a crushing weight has been removed.

The right denial of personality causes egotism to fall from one with its pride and vanity, its sensitiveness and stupidity, and the universal Self to be revealed.

He who holds to the thought, "There is no real substance to matter, the Spirit is the only true substance," finds himself no longer burdened and limited by material things. His body seems light, the things of the world do not tire him. "They that wait upon the Lord shall renew their strength; they shall mount up with wings as eagles ; they shall run, and not be weary ; and they shall walk, and not faint." Is. 40:31.

The effect of right words of denial is like water, for they cleanse, loosen, free, wash away, and dissolve false appearances. The effect of right affirmations is to fill in (fulfill), to make substantial, to build up, to establish, and cause to come into appearance that which is real and true.

The realization of true denial in thought, word, and deed is called being "born of water," and the realization of true affirmation is being "born of Spirit" This is the beginning of regeneration. He that is continually being cleansed by the word of denial "Now are ye clean through the words which I have spoken unto you" is being baptized with water. Water is the symbol of the cleansing power of repentance, change of mind, conversion, all of which come through the right denial of the world, the flesh, and the devil, or, as we have said, materiality (the world), the personal self (the flesh), and evil (the devil).

To every suggestion of evil in your daily life mentally declare, "There is no evil." To all talk of people about evil, such as scandals, descriptions of diseases, accounts of deaths, disasters, fears, discouragements and dangers, silently say, "That is not true." Many cases have been healed by that simple, silent message.

Do not feel obliged to join in conversations that dwell upon the dark side of humanity. Courtesy and good judgment will cause you to reply in ways wherein there is no offense, and yet you make no concession to evil. Silence is better than assent to error. Learn the virtue of stillness.

Copy and learn the following 1 denials, and repeat them night and morning in conjunction with the affirmations at the close of the preceding lesson :

1 Since in God there is no evil, I deny that there is any reality to evil at all.

There is no real power in sin or death.

There is no real substance to sickness or disease.

There is no true cause for sorrow.

There is nothing to fear.

2 God's world is Spiritual, not material. There is no matter, Spirit is the only substance.

3 Personality is not the real Self. The true Individual is Spirit, not flesh.

I am the free and fearless, impersonal, selfless child of God, and what I am so are you, my neighbor, as myself. Amen.

One of the happiest ways of denying for one's self is to begin your sentences with, "I am free," such as "I am free from doubt," "I am free from care," and so forth.

The denial of your personality does not destroy your Individuality, but, to the contrary, establishes it. Fear not; "He that loseth his life [loses the limited personal conception of life] for my sake [the Truth's sake] shall find it [the true Individual life]." Matt. 10:39.

LESSON III. WORDS, THEIR USE AND POWER,

GOD is supreme Intelligence, Wisdom, Understanding, Reason, all of which can be comprehended in the one word, Mind. God is Mind, and since God is the great first cause, therefore Mind is the great first cause. Divine Mind is the one creative power and source of all true manifestation.

What can be predicated of God is true of Man, who is the image and likeness of God. Man's mind is the cause of all that is in his life. Solomon says, "As he thinketh in his heart, so is he" (Prov. 23:7), and the Hindu Dhammapada expresses the same idea in the following words:

All that we are is the result of what we have thought; it is founded on our thoughts, it is made up of our thoughts. If a man speaks or acts with an evil thought, pain follows him as the wheel follows the ox that draws the cart. If a man speaks or acts with a pure thought, happiness follows him like a shadow that never leaves him.

Thoughts are the product of Mind, and the means through which Mind works. The thoughts of divine Mind are pure and good, true, and full of life and health, and they produce heavenly conditions. In the measure that man's mind dwells upon the pure and the good, he enters into health and happiness. The only real thoughts that man has are those from the Mind of God, in which is no evil imagination, memory, or production. "To think the thoughts of God after Him," as the great Kepler said, is to have a mind filled with noble, wise, loving thoughts in which there is no mixture of error or evil.

Discord and disease arise from a mixed mentality in which is belief in both good and evil as real. Pure thoughts result in pure manifestations, but mixed thoughts show forth as a mixture, an adulteration, in the bodies and circumstances of the thinkers.

The mind of man is set in order by the science of God, and all the good thoughts are gathered and ascribed to their divine source, while the beliefs in evil are separated, as the tares were taken out of the wheat in the parable (Matt. 13 : 30), and cast out into nothingness.

Divine Science and logic systematize and arrange thoughts, so that their nature is known, and name and place are given to them.

Life proves to man that a mind filled with good imagery, with peaceful, loving, gentle, trustful thoughts, is in Heaven, while one who dwells upon evil, malice, revenge, injustice, pain, and misery is in hell. For Heaven and hell are states of mind. "A good man out of the good treasure of his heart bringeth forth good things : and an evil man out of the evil treasure bringeth forth evil things." Matt. 12: 35.

All the health and happiness you have is the result of your belief in Good, which, in order to persist, must have its foundation in the true knowledge of God. If you would be constantly happy, that is, manifest your true Being which is at peace, strong and healthy, prosperous and full of love and knowledge, you must think good thoughts not only "now and then" but perpetually, which means the casting out of every other kind of thought.

We must begin to put out of our minds miserable, gloomy thoughts, not letting memories of injuries, sorrows, and mistakes possess us, and allow only those thoughts which give power and presence to Good remain in our mentality. We must put from us every doubt and fear, all discouraging thoughts of every kind, and hold fast only to those thoughts that God thinks.

Whoever is in a state of happiness is in Heaven, no matter what his surroundings may be, for Heaven is a consciousness, not a place. The Kingdom may be represented by a place filled with joy, beauty, and goodness, but primarily it is within our hearts and minds, and does not depend upon externals for perpetuation. We must find Heaven within ourselves, regardless of our associates and environments. As soon as we identify ourselves with the Divine within we become powers to externalize our inward happiness in forms which fitly symbolize God's creation. "And when he [Jesus] was demanded of the Pharisees, when the kingdom of God should come, he answered them and said, The kingdom of God cometh not with observation : neither shall they say, Lo, here ! or, lo there ! for, behold, the kingdom of God is within you." Luke 77:20, 21.

Jesus Christ came to teach men to look for Heaven right in their midst. He called his teaching "Preaching the Kingdom of Heaven," which is, in other words, declaring the ruling of the Good. At one time he contrasts it to the old preaching : "The law and the prophets were until John : since that time the kingdom of God is preached, and every man presseth into it." Luke 16:16. He declared that every nation must hear of this teaching before the end of the old conditions could come (Matt. 24:14), and he has but one instruction to all his followers as to their preaching: "As ye go, preach, saying, The kingdom of heaven is at hand." Matt. 107. What does the phrase "at hand" mean? What do you mean when in writing a letter in answer to a correspondent you say, "Your letter is at hand ?" Do you mean that it is coming by and by ? No. You mean that it is in this place at this present moment here now. So also Jesus meant: The Kingdom of Heaven is here now. Is not this the good news the gospel we are to proclaim the world over?

The Christ still says to you, "Go, preach the Kingdom of Heaven is at hand." Preach goodness and happiness as the only real presence and power (kingdom) in all the universe.

Must we speak contrary to the senses? Did not Jesus do so? With thousands of poor, hungry, sick, miserable creatures around him he still declared the true Kingdom. And while he spoke Heaven came to one after another of those cripples and miserable beings he proved his doctrine by his works.

Does it seem to you that you are telling a lie to say these things? Then remember that you are speaking of everlasting things only, and you will see that your words are true. The student of divine things ceases to think or talk about worldly and temporal appearances as though they were realities, but he lets his "conversation" be "in heaven," and enlarges upon the bright side of life, and learns to meditate upon and discuss the enduring things of Being.

When you say there is no evil, sin, sickness or death you are speaking of the real World ("My kingdom is not of this world"), where none of these things have any place.

When you say, "I am pure and holy," "I am strong and well," you are speaking of the real I, the true Self, and not of the personality called by an earthly name, and which but represents you for the time being.

Is it not written in the Scripture, "Let the weak say, I am strong" (Joel 3 :10) ?

Ignore the personal claims of sickness, believe only in the Son of God, and identify your I AM with the pure and holy, healthy, immortal Son of God. So also when speaking to others address the Real in them, and you will no longer feel that you are saying that which is not true in denying the senses, and declaring your neighbor well and strong. "Speak ye every man truth to his neighbor . . . and let none of you imagine evil in your hearts against his neighbor." Zech. 8: 16, 17. "He that speaketh truth showeth forth righteousness ... the tongue of the wise is health."Prov. 12:17, 18.

The Good is all about us and in us. We live, move, and have our being in Health, Life, and Love. God fills all things as thoughts fill the mind. But nothing comes forth without the Word. "All things were made by him [the Word] ; and without him was not anything made that was made" John 1 13.

Words are the expression of Mind. Words are thoughts made visible, or brought to consciousness and realization.

We are continually speaking words, but not always aloud, for there are silent or mental words as well as audible. These words are forming and reforming, unforming and deforming all the conditions and manifestations in and around us. If our silent or audible words dwell upon evil, then evil conditions "show forth;" if upon good, then good is manifest. "But I say unto you, That every idle [even the lightest, vainest] word that men shall speak, they shall give an account thereof ... for by thy words thou shalt be justified [established in Good] and by thy words thou shalt be condemned" [continue in ignorance and misery]. Matt. 12:36, 37.

If one says, "I am sick," "I can't understand," "I am tired," and so forth, he will continue subject to sickness, to be in ignorance, be weary, and so forth, until Truth causes him to cease from such utterances through a true change of heart.

If one says, "I will fear no evil for thou art with me" when faced by danger ; or, "I love you" before the darts of hatred and persecution ; or, "The child of God knows no failure or discouragement," he shall be established in fearlessness, in omnipotent love, in success, in just the measure that he realizes the truth of the words he utters.

The Word is the divine means by which God creates, and Man, following in the footsteps of God, uses the same means, words, to bring into manifestation what God has already created.

The original intention and use of language was not to convey thought, but for the purpose of creation. Spiritual magicians can decree a thing, and it shall be established unto them (Job 22:28).

In the Golden Age all men shall work after the manner of Christ, who did all things by his word healing the sick, raising the dead, stilling the storm, feeding the multitudes.

Jesus declared, "What things soever he [the Father] doeth, these also doeth the Son, likewise" (John 5:19), and inspiration revealed to the writer of Genesis that previous to every manifestation "God said."

"And God said, Let there be light : and there was light."

"And God said, Let there be a firmament . . . and it was so."

"And God said, Let the earth bring forth grass . . . and it was so."

"And God said, Let there be lights ... and it was so."

"And God said, Let the waters bring forth." "And God said, Let us make man in our image." Whoever follows in the footsteps of Jesus will work as he saw the Father work, speaking forth all that is to be manifest by the power of decree.

Throughout the Bible are references to God's word, its delight, and its power. Men have missed the meaning of those texts by thinking that it was the written book that was referred to, whereas the Bible itself teaches that we are to look within our hearts for the word of God and not to externals. "It is not in heaven, that thou shouldst say, Who shall go up for us to heaven, and bring it unto us, that we may hear it, and do it? Neither is it beyond the sea, that thou shouldst say, Who shall go over the sea for us, and bring it unto us, that we may hear it, and do it? But the word is very nigh unto thee, in thy mouth, and in thy heart that thou mayst do it." --Deut. 30:12-14.

It has been the inspired custom of wise men of the most spiritual nations to teach the people the holy utterances of others, that their hearts and tongues might become receptive to the divine Voice within themselves, that "well of water springing up to everlasting life." "[My words] are life unto those that find them, and health to all their flesh." Prov. 4:22.

Whoever learns where to look for divine words and believes in the holy source of inspiration within himself will realize with Jeremiah: "Thy words were found, and I did eat them, and thy word was unto me the joy and rejoicing of mine heart : for I am called by thy name, O Lord God of hosts." Jer. 15:16.

If one will read the one hundred and nineteenth Psalm with this new understanding that God's word is the Truth a living, healing presence in his own mind and that he can speak it, and so bring forth divine works, then the Scripture will become unsealed to him in many parts.

One of the forms of "speaking the word" is Prayer. As all modes of conversing unite one, more or less, according to the nature of the communication, with those whom we address, so it is with prayer. It is one means of making connection with universal Mind. A law of communion is fulfilled by right prayer, as exact a law as the one governing the transmission of electric force, or the centralizing of energy through any mechanical device.

The Soul's aspiration combined with the Mind's knowledge that what is desired is already an accomplished fact constitutes the "prayer of the righteous man that availeth much."

By prayer man acknowledges the true source of that which he desires, and the belief is turned away from its false props to the real helper.

The divine child does not beg or beseech its Heavenly Father, knowing His holy will is to give him every good thing. Prayer is not for the changing of God, who is the same yesterday, to-day, and forever, but it is for the changing of the mortal from an unbelieving and false-believing state to a consciousness like the true Mind, which knows all things to be possible to him who believes.

Thanksgiving, praise of the omnipotence and omnipresence of Good, and acknowledgment of God, lift the mind out of doubts and fears, and prepare it to cooperate in bringing to pass the very thing desired.

In order that prayer may be realization it is well to put it into an affirmative form instead of a petition. By this method the direction of Jesus is most easily fulfilled that, "What things soever ye desire, when ye pray, believe that ye receive them, and ye shall have them." Mark 11:24.

Bring the tongue under absolute and perfect control. No one can advance in spiritual unfoldment who permits the tongue to voice evil. So essential is it that the student control his lips that the very first practice enjoined by Pythagoras was a silence of five years.

James says, "If any man offend not in word, the same is a perfect man, and able also to bridle the whole body." The easiest way to bring all the body under subjection is to put a guard upon the lips, that no utterance be other than happy, peaceful, harmless, loving, kind. "I said, I will take heed to my ways, that I sin not with my tongue: I will keep my mouth with a bridle, while the wicked is before me." Ps. 39:1. "Set a watch, O Lord, before my mouth ; keep the door of my lips. " Ps. 141:3. "To him that ordereth his conversation aright will I shew the salvation of God." Ps. 50:23.

Our spoken words are the result of our silent words, therefore the thoughts must be watched continuously in order that our conversation be orderly and right. See that you do not criticize in secret, that you cease from mentally finding fault with another.

Put away all sarcasm from your speech. Never complain. Do not prophesy evil the Greeks called that blasphemy ("speaking injury" to another), and they avoided a grumbler or one who foretold misfortune because they believed he brought them bad luck.

Refrain from accusing others of hypnotism, adultery, or any other evil practices.

Withdraw all accusation from yourself. Says the Bhagavad Gita:

Upraise the self by the self, do not sink the self; for the self is the friend of the self, and even the self is the enemy of the self.

Do not let your lips form such utterances as, "I am stupid," "I hate" this and that, "I have no strength" "I am always unlucky."

Again, see that you cease from petty, false statements about your associates. It is folly to depreciate any one, for instance calling your boy "bad" or referring to the delinquencies of your partner, or calling attention to the awkwardness and rudeness of those whom we would gladly see graceful and courteous.

Have a good word for every one or else keep silent.

Accustom yourself to praying "without ceasing" by silently communing with the Good in all. Prayer is letting God think and speak through you, it is thinking God, it is God thinking. This communion with God is your very life, and the more one's mind can be filled with holy thoughts and desires the more manifestation there will be in and through one of health, prosperity, knowledge, and love.

Often breathe this prayer: "Let the words of my mouth, and the meditation of my heart, be acceptable in thy sight, O Lord, my strength, and my redeemer." Ps. 19:14. Add these words to the evening and morning repetition of affirmations and denials given in the previous lessons.

That prayer may be natural let it be free from ritualistic forms. Constancy in prayer precludes the necessity of certain external attitudes, such as kneeling, and reveals that a life filled with God-desires and God-works is more acceptable to Deity than much prostration and the recitation of many formal orisons.

"Watch ye therefore, and pray always, that ye may be accounted worthy [able] to escape all these things that shall come to pass [every calamity, disaster, disease, and death], and to stand before the Son of man" [the realization of your own sublime Divinity]. Luke 21:36.

LESSON IV. FAITH.

ONCE when the disciples of Jesus Christ were unsuccessful in healing a case that was brought to them they asked the Master what was the reason of their failure. His answer was brief, but in it lies the clue to all inability to solve the problems of life when one knows the great principles of Being, and ought to understand their application. "Jesus said unto them, Because of your unbelief: for verily I say unto you, If ye have faith as a grain of mustard seed, ye shall say unto this mountain, Remove hence to yonder place; and it shall remove; and nothing shall be impossible unto you." Matt. 17 :20.

What is the unbelief that seems to prevent the disciples of Truth from accomplishing the works? It is unbelief in one's self, in the divine power to work through one, in the presence and power of Good, of Health, and Life, and Love. It is belief in the opposites of God, in disease, death, failure, and evil generally.

The young student beginning to learn the principles of the science of God is like one who takes up the study of mathematics or music. He believes heartily in the cause which he has espoused and applies himself with assiduity to understanding and remembering its rules, but he does not expect to do well, or to be a master in his science, but by determined, faithful practice.

Nothing is promised to half-hearted service, or to a faith that is divided between Good and evil, or between Mind and matter. "He that doubteth is like the surge of the sea, driven by the wind and tossed. For let not that man think that he shall receive any thing of the Lord." Jas. 1 :6, 7 (Revised Version).

The faith that wins is that which is placed wholly in God, Spirit, Mind, as the only real substance and power. In the proportion that the student turns from believing in the reality of evil, disease, pain, and sorrow, and from believing in the power of sin, death, and materiality, he will be able to prove the healing, freeing efficacy of divine Mind.

Whoever begins to work out life's problems by divine rule is a pioneer in his own mental realm, and indeed, at the present stage of human unfoldment, he is a pioneer in the race-mind, and will need to advance with the same bravery and fidelity that distinguished those men and women who have been the first settlers and reclaimers of unknown lands in the physical sphere. The race-thoughts concerning the reality of evil are like the rocks and wild growth upon uncultivated ground the unbelieving, bigoted, malicious resistance of ignorance like the heathen Amorites and Hittites who were in possession of the fair land that was to be developed by the race obedient to God.

Steadfastness to Principle, especially in the face of the oppositions of sense and material belief, will meet the false suppositions of the race-mind, as the persistent shining of the sun upon a block of ice at last overcomes its coldness and hardness.

All your faith must be placed in God, and God alone. It will not do to have faith in the power of Good and, at the same time, believe there is some power in evil. It will not do to look to the word of God for our healing and at the same time lean upon some material aid. Continually the word of the Lord is coming to us, "Choose ye this day whom ye will serve" that is, what ye will acknowledge as the power, Good or evil, God or devil, Mind or matter, and continually we choose.

"Ye cannot serve two masters." Ye cannot serve both God and mammon. So, taking the uncompromising stand that God the Spirit is all-sufficient, the one healer, the one support and supply, the one defender and deliverer, you establish your faith, and then, no matter what comes to you, you are carried through it all-victorious.

True faith is a firm, persistent, determined belief in Almighty Good changeless, deathless, substantial Spirit as the All in All. Faith is the substance of everything that you desire. Out of your own believing is formed, that is, brought into manifestation, that which you are wishing to have. Jesus understood this law of mind, so all his teachings were to have faith, or, as he often expressed it, to believe. "Have faith in God" he said. The better translation is "Have the faith of God" Mark 11:22 (see the margin).

"For verily I say unto you, That whosoever shall say unto this mountain, Be thou removed, and be thou cast into the sea ; and shall not doubt in his heart, but shall believe that those things which he saith shall come to pass; he shall have whatsoever he saith." Mark 11:23.

"All things are possible to him that believeth." And what is this believing? Is it believing in the historical character, Jesus of Nazareth? Is it believing in a creed ? No. It is believing in your own divinity, even as Jesus believed in his. It is believing in your own words it is believing in God in you, just as Jesus believed in the Father, our God, in him.

He who would see the mountains move at his word, who would see loaves and fishes increase, and waters firm under his feet, and winds obey him, diseases fly away, sins dissolve, death succumb to his word, must not have one doubt in his heart of his divine power, must see himself one with God, so that when he speaks he sees that it is God speaking. Then indeed shall he believe that those things that he saith shall come to pass, because he lets God speak the word in him he does not look at the personality as himself and true indeed is it of him that he shall have whatsoever he saith.

What is God's faith? It is faith in Himself, because He knows there is none else in whom to have faith. Have faith in yourself. Have faith in God in you. God is your own true Self. God, the Son, and God, the Father, are one and the same. God in you is the only power and presence. God in all is the Reality of all. God is the only one in your neighbor. God is the only one you trust.

There are times in the on-going of the spiritual student when he is brought face to face with hard problems and strange situations. Then it may be that evil seems more real to you than usual, that here is a place where the Word does not seem to act with its customary effect, and doubts begin to creep in, and you feel that you are being forsaken. Then is the time when you show your steadfastness, then you prove yourself to yourself, then, just at such times, you show your faith in Good as the only real presence and divine Mind as the all-sufficient power. Such times in the Truthseeker's experience have been described as a clashing of Truth and error, the error trying to hold its ground while the Truth steadily and firmly establishes itself. It is the warring of the flesh against the Spirit, and the Spirit overcoming. The Truth does not fight, neither does the Spirit, but it is error apparently struggling as though it feels that its time is short, and the student must keep still and see the bloodless, silent, sure victory of the Good, of Health, of Life, of Truth.

It has always been in the history of the world that whenever a great truth has been given to it, the world fights it; but those who do not let themselves be influenced by fear or doubt, but have the courage of their convictions and stand by their principles, no matter who wars against them, finally find themselves upon the victorious side.

Even in what are called material truths there is seldom any great discovery given to the world that it will accept at once. How Galileo was fought! How Columbus was laughed at and talked to to discourage him! And how he held out! The last days of his voyage, just before the discovery, when the sailors were very desperate and threatening mutiny if Columbus would not turn back, are a good example of those days that sometimes seem to come to the student of Truth when he is urged by circumstances, by doubts, by his senses, by personality, to give up his stand and throw aside his principles ;

then is he to have faith in his God, even as Columbus had in himself and his expedition, and God who promises all things to them that trust Him will never fail him.

If one says he has no faith, he is mistaken. All have faith, for Faith is God.

The only question is, what have you been having faith in? Has it been in disease, that it is strong and persistent, and will require years to heal, or else is incurable ?

When seeking satisfaction, what have you put your faith in? Whisky? When looking for power, what have you believed in? Money? Our faith has been scattered and dissipated amongst a thousand false gods, and all that we have been putting into evils and into material things must be gathered and concentrated in God.

There is no unbelief
Whoever plants a seed beneath the sod,
And waits to see it push away the clod,
Trusts he in God.

There is no unbelief
The heart that looks on when the eyelids close,
And dares to live when life has only woes,
God's comfort knows.

There is no unbelief,
And still by day and night, unconsciously,
The heart lives by that faith the lips deny
God knoweth why.

Lizzie York Case.

Your faith is your life. If one's faith is in a power that is limited then the life seems limited, and why place your faith in anything less than omnipotence?

All that the Truth teaches is to put your faith in the Supreme and not in any thing or any power less than God. You take the faith which you have placed in medicines, opiates, liniments, canes and crutches, eye-glasses, trusses, tonics, and so forth ("gods of wood and stone"), and give it to Spirit alone, believing God supports you, God invigorates you, God is your seeing power and health; and then you do not compromise in any way. To try to serve two masters, trusting the Spirit to heal you, and looking to the smallest particle of matter, even to a glass of water, for your healing is that mistake which is called in the Scripture "idolatry." And the result is only partial healing, or being healed only to get sick again.

Now we wish absolute healing; we desire only chat healing which is of God, the Highest, that healing that is everlasting. Looking to powers that are unreliable and changeable brings results that are unreliable and changeable. That is the reason why the practice of medicine can never be a science. It is largely theoretical and experimental "empiricism" they call it.

There is but One Physician that never fails when we trust Him completely. We place all our trust in the unlimited Healer, and the result to us is unlimited Health.

If any look to a limited power for healing, such as materia medica, substance less than the divine Substance, material which is not God; or mesmerism, a will-power less than the divine Will, and even contrary to it ; or magnetism, an emanation said to be from the human body, but limited, often evil in other words, an emanation less than the divine Essence ; or to mediumship, a control by what are called spirits, said to be inferior to the Most High, the One Spirit, these will be but slightly healed. 'They have healed also the hurt of the daughter of my people slightly" (Jer. 6:14), because they look to other gods than the One God.

"And Asa in the thirty and ninth year of his reign was diseased in his feet, until his disease was exceeding great : yet in his disease he sought not to the

LESSON V. KNOWLEDGE AND GOOD JUDGMENT.

FAITH and understanding go hand in hand when the works of the Christ are made manifest. Whenever either appears alone there comes a limitation in healing, for each is essential to the full manifestation of the other.

The belief in faith alone, commonly called "blind faith," in which the disciple does not seek knowledge, degenerates into superstition and eventually becomes barren. Increase of faith comes through increase of knowledge ("I know whom I have believed" 2 Tim. 1:12), and the student who seeks to add to his consciousness of healing power must apply himself to a fervent and systematic study of divine Mind and its idea.

Misunderstanding of the character and office of God and His child, Man, is the cause of impotency in accomplishing divine works. Many a faith-healer has lost a case because of this lack of knowledge of God's wish concerning the one for whom he is praying. Perhaps he has prayed earnestly, and is near the state of consciousness whereby the false claim of disease can be met and vanquished when a tempting doubt begins to insinuate itself into his mind :

"Perhaps it is not the will of God that this one shall be healed; perhaps his time has come to die."

Then the ardor of the petitioner begins to cool. He is shaken. He fears to proceed lest he be doing that which is contrary to the divine will. He weakens, he ceases to pray, and the patient goes "the way of all flesh."

"The prayer of faith shall save the sick, and the Lord shall raise him up." Jas. 5:15. But the faith that always succeeds must be founded upon the knowledge that it is not the will of God that any man shall die. The world has hypnotized itself too long upon this subject, and must now be awakened to the truth that God does not send death any more than He sends sin. "The wages of sin is death ; but the gift of God is eternal life." Rom. 6:23. "I have no pleasure in the death of him that dieth, saith the Lord God : wherefore turn yourselves, and live ye." Eze. 18:32.

"God is not the author of confusion, but of peace." 1 Cor. 14:33. God is not the author of discord, such as disease and death. Ignorance is the cause of all evil manifestations, and the grossest ignorance of all is to ascribe their origin to God. Let us be healed of this ignorance.

Solomon says, "Wisdom is the principal thing ; therefore get wisdom : and with all thy getting get understanding." Prov. 4:7.

"This is life eternal, that they might know thee the only true God, and Jesus Christ, whom thou hast sent" (John 17:3), breathed that Master of knowledge who had the key to all power the only true God and perfect Man, His child." All true knowledge takes its rise in this primum mobile of understanding, the Unity of God and the Divinity of Man.

God and Man are to be studied and thoroughly known, and thus shall the problems of life be solved, and eternal health and happiness be ours.

The mind must be fully imbued with the foundation principles of this teaching in order to receive and assimilate the lessons that are their logical sequence.

The basic propositions, briefly reviewed, can be stated as follows:

1 Since God, the Good, is all, evil has no real place or power.

2 Since Man, God's child, is divine, the carnal self has no real place or power.

3 Since God's World is spiritual substance, materiality has no real place or power.

Those semblances of consciousness called "carnal sense" and the "human intellect" naturally rebel against one or more of these statements, for spiritual things are spiritually discerned. But there is an inner teacher called the Intuition that will calmly and steadily hold to their truth until at last fretting, resisting mortal will yields, and the God-wisdom (the divine sophia of Paul, Solomon, and the other wise ones) has its way. Paul expresses this very clearly in 1 Corinthians, second chapter, and also James, in James, third chapter, thirteenth to eighteenth verses, which passages the student will please read and ponder.

True understanding comes from within. "There is a spirit in man : and the inspiration of the Almighty giveth them understanding." Job 32:8. Only God can teach us Truth. And since Man is the image of Omniscience, within him is all knowledge, and the Spirit of Truth is his true instructor. The most that an external teacher can do is to point to this inner teacher and train the student to become receptive to instruction from his own Soul.

The best educators of the day tell us that all one will ever know is already in him was in him even as a child, as the oak is in the acorn. Books, travel, and other externals are but suggestions which serve to uncover and draw out the knowledge that is within.

By seeking the highest wisdom of all, that of divine Mind, all other knowledge will be added. Being filled with spiritual knowledge does not exclude an understanding of the things of the world, just as knowing about the sun does not prevent our knowing about its reflection in the sea.

Through prayer men and women have come, even suddenly, to the ability to read, to compute numbers, to understand foreign tongues. By faithfully believing in the inner Teacher students have had the arts of worldly wisdom given them, becoming correct in speech, astute in reasoning, excelling in music and painting, through seeking the Highest. "And the Jews marvelled, saying, How knoweth this man letters, having never learned ?" John 7:15. "And all that heard him [Jesus] were astonished at his understanding and answers." Luke 2:47. "Daniel answered and said, Blessed be the name of God forever and ever : for wisdom and might are his: . . . he giveth wisdom unto the wise, and knowledge to them that know understanding." Dan. 2:20, 21.

Divine knowledge is self-increasing. He who claims knowledge for himself will have knowledge added, but he who reiterates, "I don't know," and "I can't understand," thus denying Wisdom, will be denied (Matt. 10:33).

"Take heed therefore how ye hear: for whosoever hath, to him shall be given" Luke 8:18. Let us get more understanding by dwelling often upon what we do already know, and to every question that comes into mind respond silently, "I understand, I know the answer." Then it will come to pass that the faithful student will find his teachers coming to him, books will open to the places wherein the information lies, and he can learn from everybody and everything, finding tongues in trees, books in the running brooks, Sermons in stones, and good in everything.

The Truth student who does not depend upon external teachers and books finds all life in collusion to advance him in the understanding of things real and unreal, educating him both within and without.

The Scriptures become an open book to those who listen to the Spirit of Truth. Inspiration is not limited to a few souls. All are inspired, for inspiration is the breath of God, by which man lives. Every good thought is an inspiration, no matter how commonplace and trite it may be.

True prophets and spiritual seers are the result of ardent search after spiritual light. To breathe in and forth thoughts of good continually manifests the mind of Christ and gives the power to interpret Scripture, causing it to bless, feed, and instruct in divine things, according to its holy intention.

The Bible is a rich storehouse of Truth, but it takes the Mind that inspired it to give its meaning. Therefore intellectual effort cannot remove the veil without the co-operation of the spiritual Mind.

There is a Correspondence between things natural and things spiritual which is revealed to the wise one, and this not only opens the eyes to a right reading of Scripture, but also causes all nature to reveal herself as a great symbolism of the processes of thought and the laws of Mind.

In symbolism men and women represent dominant ideas in mind; divisions of the earth, mountains, islands, seas, signify states of mind ; trees, rocks, animals, stand for traits of character.

The Bible from Genesis to Revelation is an account of man's spiritual ongoing as a race and as an individual from the time he rises above the "dust of the ground" (Gen. 2:7), or from the common lot of humanity, to the day in which he is given a name above every earthly name (Rev. 2:17; 22:4) and stands a proven Son of the Most High.

The divine science of correspondence has been greatly uncovered through the light of the seer, Swedenborg. It has always been the language of the prophets (Jer. 1:1-14; Eze. 37:16-21; Heb. 8:5; Gal. 4: 22-31), and of poets and sages. "And without a parable spake he not unto them" Matt. 13:34. "When he, the Spirit of truth, is come, he shall guide you into all truth ... for he shall receive of mine and shew it unto you." John 16:13, 14.

Spiritual transactions must be translated into the language of mortal-sense that they be understood, so as to be of practical benefit to mortals who desire to be redeemed from mortality.

The Truth has always been in the world, but the fear and intolerance of men have kept it hid; also the intoxication of earthly pursuits has blinded their eyes to its holy joys. But now the race is rapidly awakening from its dream that satisfaction can be found in worldly pleasures, and the age is ripe for the fullest presentation of God's Truth.

The mind that accepts the whole Truth regardless of consequences and independent of the fears of man comes to judgment, that divine faculty by which he discriminates between good and evil, the spiritual and material, the divine and carnal. The process of separating the false from the true begins in his mentality and life, and he has the good sense or good judgment to hold fast to the eternally good and utterly refuse the evil.

The Day of Judgment is revealed to be a continuous day, now ruling our lives and casting out error. "Now is the judgment of this world : now shall the prince of this world be cast out." John 12:31. "Because the prince of this world is judged." John 16:11. It is the presence of God's good judgment in the heart of the devotee. The wheat is separated from the tares, the truth from the error, the sheep from the goats, the spiritual traits from the carnal, the positive from the negative, each being put in its true place.

The day of judgment is a welcome day, for by good judgment comes knowledge of this mixed world of appearances in which good and evil seem so commingled, the divine and the human so interwoven, truth and error so confused as to justly merit the appellation, an "adulterous [or adulterated] generation" (Mark 8:38). All uncertainty vanishes before this divine ability to distinguish the real from the unreal, the genuine from the counterfeit.

It is promised that the Christ will work with us until this power of judgment is established in the heart of each, for when that is accomplished, then righteousness shall reign without end. "He shall not fail nor be discouraged, till he have set judgment in the earth." "For when thy judgments are in the earth, the inhabitants of the world will learn righteousness." "And the work of righteousness shall be peace; and the effect of righteousness quietness and assurance forever." Is. 42:4; 26:9; 32:17.

Socrates says, "If you would teach the people to act rightly, teach them to form correct judgments." In this world of opposites we must know that the good is the positive and the evil is the negative ; the first is the real, the second is the opposite to real.

To the question, "What is the origin of evil?" there is but one direct answer: It has no origin. It is nothing, and it came from nothing. It has no substance, it is without principle, it is pure negation.

If we give evil origin and reality, then we must say that God created it, for He made all things that are made. In a sense we can say that that which is the origin of good is the cause of its opposite, just as the carpenter who builds a house is the cause of the shadow which the house casts. In that sense the prophet, who seeing evil as much a reality as good was not in the full Truth, declares, "I form the light and create darkness : I make peace and create evil : I the Lord do all these things" (Is. 45:7), but the highest revelation says, "This then is the message which we have heard of him, and declare unto you, that God is light, and in him is no darkness at all" I John 1:5.

Evil is darkness, without being or law except to the mind not fully instructed in Truth. This mind, still in the valley of shadows, reasons from a basis of relative truths in which there is satisfaction for a time, but soon new questions as baffling as the old arise, and no complete satisfaction comes until the wise one takes the absolute stand: Evil is pure nothingness; absolutely without place, law, or origin.

In the childhood of our spiritual advancement the mind is content with such explanations as: "A lie is but a truth perverted ; evil is but undeveloped good." But the maturer student soon demands, "How can the Good that is God have ever been imperfect or undeveloped? Good has always been good, it never was evil. Either make the tree good and its fruit good, or make it evil and its fruit evil (Matt. 12:33). Who is this that lies? or perverts good? Who is this that makes mistakes, and is in ignorance?"

Absolute Truth compels its adherent to acknowledge that since God, the one Mind, is the only real thinker such error-thinking is but supposition and truly unthought. As a prophet of the new age has voiced it :

The dreamer and dream are one, for neither is true or real. Mrs. M. B. G. Eddy.

God is not the unknowable, but that which is the opposite of God, the realm of evil, sin, sickness, sorrow, and death is the unknowable. It has been decreed from eternity that evil should not be known, and to attempt to know it is the first delusion of mortal minds. The belief of Adam and Eve that they could disobey and thwart, or prevent, the fulfillment of God's will represents the first step of self-deception, followed by others until the delinquent reaches the climax of delusions, death.

The tree of the knowledge of good and evil is like the mirage of the desert, fair to look upon and harmless as long as one knows its nature to be illusion, a play, a game, nothing in itself. But when one does not listen to the inner Guide, but begins to make something out of nothing, he thinks he can eat of this tree. He never does eat of it. God's law is never broken he who thinks he can break it thinks he can suffer, grow sick, and die, which he does again and again, until after bitter experience he turns to the Truth and begins his journey out of the land of dreams.

The best that can be known of evil is that it is not to be known, and that to try to know it is fruitless and useless.

As soon as a shadow is understood in its relation to the thing casting it the mind quickly dismisses all thought about it. It excites no wonder, it brings no fear. The way to make it disappear or change form and place is understood, and the mind applies its study and mastery in the right direction.

Materiality is the shadow of spirituality. Physical manifestation at its best is but the reflection of the real substantial creation of God. This reflection is good or ill according to the state of the reflector, the human mind, which, if clear and still like a calm, limpid lake, can give forth an image worthy of the divine Reality.

"The world is what we make it," and "We take out of the world what we put into it" are sayings of wisdom.

Clearness and the power to be still become the properties of the human mind as it conforms itself to the divine Mind, and confesses it to be the only real Mind. Then comes the true negativeness in which is reflected the true Self as it is in God.

Nature is the mirror of God ; the receptivity of manifestation ; the deep over which the Spirit of God ever moves, bringing forth His image; the "emptiness" or vacuum; the nothing being perpetually filled with the All.

The true Kingdom, which is the fullness of manifestation, is here in all its completeness. Whoever seeks its joys and treasures, and strives to understand its laws and purposes, will also come into the knowledge and possessions of this world which shadows it. "Seek ye the kingdom of God; and all these things shall be added unto you." Luke 12:31.

To follow after the riches and wisdom of a world of change and decay is the act of one who tries to possess and control a shadow without any knowledge of or hold upon the object back of it. Read I Kings, third chapter, ninth to fourteenth verses.

Right judgment teaches to divide the true Self from the carnal. The wisdom of God guides us to seek first the real Man in every person, to hold that one ever in mind, to love that one and believe in him. Then we know how to regard the performances of the fleshly self, the persona. We are not surprised, or pained, or disappointed by it. We neither criticize unjustly nor condemn. We see no personality as wholly bad, or believe in total depravity.

Our judgment is just, and the false is uncovered but for the purpose of causing it to disappear under the healing influences of the Sun of Truth.

The Eastern sage traces all false appearance to what he calls "nescience" not-knowing or ignorance.

True knowledge combines in it every divine manifestation, such as love, faith, goodness, power, and therefore contains the secret of all healing and redeeming. "The wisdom that is from above is first pure, then peaceable, gentle, and easy to be entreated, full of mercy and good fruits, without partiality, and without hypocrisy." Jas. 3:17.

Meditate upon Scriptural passages while holding that you have the Mind of God and that He makes you understand what He has inspired.

Watch that your lips and your thoughts do not assert, "I don't know" and "I can't understand." It is true that the carnal mind does not know the things of

God and "not that we are sufficient of ourselves to think anything" (2 Cor.3:5) if we are speaking from the earthly standpoint. But we are not. Our purpose is to train our believing into our divine Self and keep our "I" lifted up above the earth.

Learn to look upon all things material, personal, or evil as but signs and symbols back of which lie the Real, to be found and expressed, or drawn out, by the God Man in us.

Some mentalities seem to leap quickly out of their former errors into the Truth. It is because of the difference in beliefs that the unfolding appears so different. Some let go of their errors immediately, and some cling to old thoughts even though earnestly desiring to drop them, fear, conventionality, or one of the causes mentioned by Jesus (Matt. 13:21 ; Luke 8:14) seeming to prevent their progress.

Be true and possess your souls in patience. Realization will come. Only be faithful. What you consciously hold to-day sinks deep into the sub-conscious realm where lie these false memories and habits of thinking, and persistent right believing will at last displace the old mind and substitute for the untrue the true.

The renewing of our minds may be compared to the change which comes to one who has been, journeying for months upon the sea, until his senses are charged with the motion of the ship. When he steps upon terra firma it may be for days that the land will seem to rock and roll, but he continually remembers the truth concerning his environment and himself, until at last his consciousness is normal, and he is at rest.

LESSON VI. UNITY AND CONCENTRATION.

THE pursuit of Truth uncovers the spiritual discernment by which men clearly see that all real good is one, and this intuitive perception of the unity of the true is confirmed by the logical processes of reason. These two witnesses, Intellect and Intuition, establish the Truth in our hearts, and wherever inspiration is corroborated by reason there is the Rock against which no doubts or fears of mortal sense can prevail.

All Good is one and the same. In the highest, love, wisdom, health, purity, and every manifestation of Good are one in essence and in being. It is only to mortal sense and its misconceptions of life that love and wisdom ever seem separate, that justice and mercy stand apart, that innocence and knowledge are disunited, that health and goodness are not companions.

Perfect Good includes all good. The true Life is a whole life with nothing in it of death or disease. Divine Health is wholeness, or holiness, in Spirit, soul and body.

Absolute Truth is one there cannot be two truths contradicting each other, else one of them would not be the whole truth.

All good can be gathered under one name, God, who is all that is good and the good of all. The one God of us all is the one good of us all, to which men have given an infinite variety of names, such as Intelligence, Prosperity, Right, Freedom, besides deific names, such as Brahm, Jupiter, and Jehovah. "That which exists is one: sages call it variously." Rigveda. "There shall be one Lord, and his name one." Zech. 14 :9.

The spiritual Mind is ever uniting. It seeks God in everybody and everything, and makes that the point of oneness with all. It operates by love. "I drew them with bands of love." Hos. 11:4. Whenever there is dislike or in-harmony, its source can be found in the carnal mind. According to Max Muller this is the way we can know which mind is operating in us:

The carnal mind and the spiritual mind are seen to act in this way: the carnal always detects differences while the spiritual notes similarities.

The tendency of the human intellect is to differentiate, and this tendency can be checked by not enlarging upon the differences between those manifestations of God which are one, such as Spirit, Soul, and Mind. If we see the identity of these in the Highest we can clearly analyze the appearance of difference to the human mind, and disclose that it is but a matter of the point of view from which these things are seen, or perhaps a difference in the use of terms.

The broad, deep mind can see the unity of all religions and expressions of Truth. It is waste of time and distracting to thought to seek and tell the differences between the beliefs of mankind. Let us be content to find the good and the true in every teacher and his teaching. Then if it ever devolves upon us to point out a stumbling stone we can, like Jesus, do it impersonally and with authority.

Universal tolerance finds Truth omnipresent, and has no respect of persons, creeds, or institutions, yet gives true deference to the real of each.

The purpose of religion is to unite God and Man, and that is the true religion which breaks down the barriers between man and his fellow-beings, and brings to him the consciousness of the eternal union between the Heavenly Father and His Child. The origin of the word "religion" is two Latin words meaning "to bind together again." The power of reconciliation' which is in the true religion is without limit, joining together those which have seemed hopelessly apart, even at enmity, such as the higher and lower natures. It is the Christ-truth that breaks down "the middle wall of partition" between the human nature and the divine by causing the mortal to become obedient to the true Self. Then, overshadowed by the real Man, the earthly is "adopted" into the same inheritance of health and age-lasting life.

It is Truth that forms the universal brotherhood by showing we are all one Body and one Spirit (Eph. 4:4) in God, and that what is done to the least in that Body is done to the whole. The great atonement (atone-ment) is brought about by the sacrifice of the old nature, the selfish one, and the glorifying of the true Self, who ever seeks the good of the whole.

The true Self of man is God, for since God is All in All and there is none else, man has no being but God. The Mind of God and its Idea are one. For, since God is the only mind, there can be no thought or idea in it but what is God, and He, Himself, all there is to think upon.

As mortals, men can only reflect God. Reflectors of a light are not the light itself. A reflection has no substance and is not the thing it reflects, so that mortal man cannot say, "I am God."

Divine Man is identical with God. "I and my Father are one," says Christ, the divine Man (John 10:30), but "I go unto the Father: for my Father is greater than I," says Jesus, the perfect human concept and the reflection of the Christ (John 14:28).

Jesus Christ combined in himself all the steps, the teachings, and the means by which humanity can perfectly reflect God, and by which the real Man may be proven identical with its divine source. The Christ is the Lord, the God of the whole earth and Spirit of us all. Jesus was the man in whom was out-pictured the true relation between the human ego and the divine. In him was portrayed the crucifixion (the crossing-out or cancellation) of the old man followed by the vindication and resurrection of the regenerate or new Man, which is finally transmuted and absorbed into its original Self, God and very God.

Through an impersonal, selfless life Jesus became identified with humanity as a whole, and his history is prophecy and promise of its achievements, both in the individuals and in the race. Whoever unites himself in heart and mind with Jesus Christ will find out the shortest, most direct road to unity with his own true Being, the Self who is his God and God of us all.

Jesus Christ cannot be exalted too high in the minds of men, even to God of all being. For while men elevate this Man they are lifting up all humanity, for eventually all who see the Godhood of Jesus will see God in themselves.

Concentration is the divine art of centering the mind upon what we please as long as we please. This power is only attained by making God, spiritual realities, the continual object of our thoughts. The appearance of concentration which seems to be developed when one has a standard less than the Most High is only the acquirement of a fixed habit of thinking which is the reverse of true concentration, for it lacks the pliability and elasticity which is essential to the well-rounded thinking, and which only comes through focusing upon the Universal.

Men concentrate upon money so that their faculties are very acute and alert respecting money-making. But take their business away from them, as is generally done some time in their lives either through circumstances, or because of age, or someone's loving though mistaken zeal to bless them with leisure and with other pursuits, and dissolution begins both mentally and physically, for they cannot center upon anything else. Thus it is with the professor, the artist, the actor, the society woman, the busy housewife, or anyone of ardent temperament who intensely concentrates all his energies and desires upon anything less than the absolute Truth. So also with the religionist who mixes error with his Truth ; nevertheless if he be sincere, fearless, and meek he will be led to the Great Truth, God, which to meditate upon and love with your whole being clarifies the mind, purifies the passions, and gives that power of self-management that knows no limit in usefulness, peace, and happiness.

Truth has its science and its art, and concentration is that art. There is no religion extant but has its methods of concentration. The Hindu calls it yoga; the Christian, "prayer." Christ gives it as a command : "Watch ye therefore, and pray always." Luke 21:36.

Practical Christianity requires complete devotion, entire consecration of all you are and all you have to the cause and manifestation of Truth. Concentration is the method by which this is accomplished.

Everything that appears to be external to you should suggest to you Spirit, God, Good, Heaven, Truth. Learn to translate all your employments, your instruments, the people you meet, the things you see, into the spiritual ideas for which they stand.

Human beings are each symbols of Truth one a personification of Joy, another of Strength, another of Peace, another of Prosperity, according to the relationships they are bearing to you at the time you meet them. Your employments represent the operations that your Spirit is engaged in at the time you are working. If you are sweeping a room, meditate upon the Truth that sweeps error from your mental house. If you are sewing a garment, think of the manifestation of right and good which your Spirit desires shall clothe the Soul for whom you are working. If you are building a house, image the true temple, and with every nail drive home a truth that will show forth the Kingdom of Heaven. If you are teaching children, see them as precious expressions of Mind, your own thoughts being trained as fit habitants of the divine realm. If you deal with people in buying and selling, meet them as representatives of the Christ, and so develop patience, sweetness, genuine deference, and integrity. Knead love into the bread you bake, wrap strength and courage in the parcel you tie for the woman with the weary face, hand trust and candor with the coin which you pay the man with the suspicious eyes.

Preach the gospel with your every gesture and glance through right practice of concentration.

The human mind in which every thought is purified and directed with clearness upon the one theme, God, becomes like a clear, calm lake, which reflects perfectly whatever is upon its surface. Then any thought that is held before it can be imaged with exactness and truth, as one sees oneself in a flawless mirror.

Perfect concentration is having the "single eye" spoken of by Jesus "If thine eye be single thy whole body shall be full of light" (Matt. 6:22), and the "one-pointed"' mind described by Krishna (Bhagavad Gita 6:12).

The great-souled ones, united to godlike nature, knowing Me to be the exhaustless origin of all things, worship Me with mind that turns to nothing else. Bhagavad Gita 9:13.

There are many methods of practicing spiritual concentration ; some are external and others internal, but all have for their nucleus the idea of God.

Sages agree that the easiest and most direct practice is the internal, through governing the thoughts and desires with silent words of Spirit.

True concentration results in the restoration of the memory, for the mind then has the power to select what thoughts it desires and to hold them as long as it wills. By ability to focus the thoughts comes the power to focus the eyes, and the sight is renewed ; through mastery over the faculty of attention the mechanism of the ears again obeys the will, and hearing is regained.

We become like that which we concentrate upon, and the more at-one we are with it the more we know it. All study is concentration, and true education gives us power to know a thing by our becoming it for the time being the essence and very heart of it.

Sir Isaac Newton when asked by what means he had been able to develop his system of the universe said : "By making it incessantly the subject of my thoughts."

Enthusiasm is one of the essential concomitants to successful concentration, that is, that which manifests in works of Christ. No one can be too enthusiastic in seeking divine knowledge and believing in the possibilities of the true One within him.

Every great and commanding movement in the annals of the world is the triumph of enthusiasm. Emerson,

"If ye know these things, happy are ye if ye do them." John 13:17.

That Christianity is but theoretical which puts off the fruits of Truth until a future life. Too long has the great doctrine of Jesus been betrayed by those who declare his inspired injunctions, such as "Be ye perfect," "Resist not evil," "Love your enemies" too transcendental and impracticable. He meant what he said, and he knew the fulfillment to be possible and inseparable from the complete Christ-life. He drew no limit at any command as to thought, speech, or works, but expected that all who believed in the Truth would do the same as he did.

We have an example in the life of Jesus Christ of what are the fruits of a unity with God. He who enters a life of practical Christianity should expect to comply with all the directions Christ gives to his followers, among which are: "Preach the gospel, heal the sick, cleanse the lepers, raise the dead, cast out devils : freely ye have received, freely give." Matt. 10:7,8.

The goal that Truth places before us is the same attainment reached by Jesus Christ. And if we cannot yet do all the works he did, because of our ignorance or our unbelief, let us at least have the loyalty of the devoted students of an earthly art or science, such as music or mathematics, who do not deny that man can accomplish the great things of their study, and who judge of their own proficiency and knowledge by their ability to put into practice the principles they have espoused.

Among the first works to be performed by a student of Christ are those of bodily healing. While there is an A B C of this divine art there is also an X Y Z, and Jesus shows us that some cases yield easily, while others require closer practice and greater realization, as in the case of the obsessed child (Matt. 17). In mathematics the power to count and to add belongs to its infant study, but even the most complicated problem includes these first practices. In the same way healing runs throughout the whole process of regeneration, and we shall never be finished with these primary steps until we have ceased altogether to function in the realm of mortal problems.

All divine manifestation is allied to healing, and he who masters the principles and practices of the healing of the body through the word of Truth will also have the key to soul-healing, called "salvation," and healing of circumstances, called "prosperity." The Hebrew and Greek words translated "salvation" and "health'" in the Bible are often the same. Paul taught the three-fold healing, and prayed for his converts that "your whole spirit and soul and body be preserved blameless unto the coming of our Lord Jesus Christ." I Thes. 5:23.

Permanent health conies through freeing the mind from its ignorance and sin. Unless one ceases from sin he cannot be free from sickness, and if men do not know the Principle (God) of Healing, their cure will be temporal, or they will fall into some other disease. The dependence of the body upon the soul for its health is an old teaching. We find Plato telling the Greek physicians that the cause of their failure to heal was in their ignorance of the needs of the soul.

Neither ought you to attempt to cure the body without the soul; for the reason why the cure of many diseases is unknown to the physicians of Hellas is because they are ignorant of the whole, which ought to be studied also, for the part can never be well unless the whole is well.

For over three hundred years after the advent of Jesus his followers combined healing works with their preaching, and considered them to be the signs which should follow (Mark 16:17, 18) and confirm the truth of the doctrines (Mark 16:20). But when quarrels and schisms began to disrupt the church, then pride, worldly ambition, and covetousness seemed to hide the simple teachings of the meek and lowly One. Nevertheless the healing has never been quite abolished, and now that its principle is being grasped by reason as well as faith, it has come to abide forever, and will shine "more and more unto the perfect day." Prov. 4:18.

Every lover of Truth who embodies in himself the unity of the principles and the works of Christ is one who' is a center of healing for all the world, the light of the world, the salt of the earth. Universal healing radiates from him as rays from the sun, and many are healed by simply looking towards him for healing.

Virtue goes forth from him even when personally he is not conscious of it.

Success in healing is proportionate to the knowledge you have of Truth, the depth of your love, and the trueness of your life. Cases are healed quickly or slowly according to the receptivity of the patient, the nature of your own beliefs, and your realization of the Truth you are giving.

The daily living in spiritual concentration is working for "that meat which endureth unto everlasting life" (John 6:27), and "laying up treasures in heaven" (Matt. 6:20). "Therefore every scribe which is instructed unto the kingdom of heaven is like unto a man that is an householder, which bringeth forth out of his treasure things new and old." Matt. 13:52.

The realm in which lie the spiritual treasures of the Christ-living and healing is called by the Psalmist, The Secret Place of the Most High (Ps. 91). The modern name that has been given to it is The Silence. Jesus refers to it in the words "in secret," used in Matthew, sixth chapter, fourth, sixth, and eighteenth verses. It is there we are enjoined to commune with the Father, and what He hears in secret He will manifest openly.

The student should be able to dwell in the secret place ever, even when outwardly living a most ordinary life. Many saints attained this power. Brother Lawrence, who lived two centuries ago, had the key to this peace, and gave it very plainly to those who sought him, as we read in the booklet, The Practice of the Presence of God.

In order to develop this power of meditation it is recommended to the student to make an appointment with your inner Self at a regular time each day and enter into the silence of your heart and mind, shutting the doors of the senses (Matt. 6:6), and to meditate upon some spiritual truth with which you especially desire to be at-one.

When once the joy of this peace-bringing practice is realized new methods of soul-communion will be revealed to you by the Spirit of Truth within which you evoke by this devotion, and which is itself the inexhaustible well of Truth.

For a beginner a half-hour daily meditation, such as is herewith suggested, will be sufficient:

1 Select a spiritual theme, such as Love, Peace, Purity, or some other name of Good. It need not be the same one every day.

2 Mentally repeat it seven times. To avoid counting divide the seven thus: three, and three, and one. The theme is a seed and you plant it in the mental soil of your human thinking by this process of repetition.

3 Then let your thoughts go. Let the thought-seed send out rootlets into your mind and grow. As long as your mind dwells upon spiritual things you are in right meditation, which leads to concentration. The stems, branches, leaves, flowers, and fruit may not resemble the seed, but they are all one, and united by the one life. So are all spiritual thoughts one with each other, because Divinity is one.

4 But if your vine begins to put out a branch that does not bear fruit to the Good, or to Spirituality, you must cut it off. That is, if the mind begins to wander to material things, or to evil, or to unspiritual events and people, or to sleep, these are branches you cut off instantly by repeating the word which is your theme seven times, as in 2, and again letting your mind go, as in 3.

Write in a blank book kept for the purpose some of the principal thoughts that come to you in the silence, or, if you keep this half-hour in company with other Truth-seekers express aloud the Truths (not visions or speculations) that you have received, as Jesus said (Matt. 10:27). For if you express what Truth you receive, you will receive more Truth to express. "For whomsoever hath, to him shall be given." Luke 8:18.

PART II.

LESSON VII. OUR HEREDITY, AND FREEDOM FROM SENSUALITY.

HEREIN is my Father glorified, that ye bear much fruit." John 15:8. One of the fruits of the Tree of Life (Rev. 22 12) is Healing, and among the glories of practical Christianity are the thousands of sick and pain-stricken humanity that are being healed through its ministry every day.

These lessons are to make healers, and every one who receives these teachings thoroughly and practices faithfully the exercises given must ever hold himself in readiness to heal whoever applies to him in a true spirit and shows a willingness to do his part.

All can heal. Whoever can speak Truth can heal. Every true word spoken is a healing force sent out into the world, and specific healing is simply a gathering together of healing words, and sending them in the direction that one pleases (Luke 7:8, 9), charging them with an especial mission in bringing forth a definite result, just as steam is generated by the universal action of the sun upon water, but does not do an exact work for man until it is concentrated, held, and given direction by some mechanism which is the result of man's inventive genius or discovery.

Love makes the truest, most successful healers, and wherever we find "natural healers" we find lovers of humanity. Their power has its source in the same spring whence flows every good, and it is because of their great love-nature that certain students are such powers for healing from their very entrance into life. Its warm radiance has been called "magnetism," but when they turn from looking to their personal presence to do the healing and look to their word they find the quality that healed was mental, not physical.

All healing is from God, whether the means used have been the relics of superstition or the skill of the most advanced practitioner in medical arts .

We shall learn that the material means and other methods in which there is no recognition of God were but an interference, and caused the health to seem temporal instead of eternal, as it should be.

If we look into the secret causes of the success of worldly doctors and nurses we shall find them to be either love or faith, and generally both. The physician who grows old in a practice that is an honor to him is, deep down in his heart, an earnest lover of his fellow beings, one whose love has caused him to make many a sacrifice of his own comfort and pleasure, and often to give faithful service where he knew there was no money to pay him. Happy is that physician if he discovers the true power that has been back of his work. Other successful physicians, though seeming to have little love, have great faith in their method, their school, themselves. So it is with spiritual healers love and faith are the two principal elements of success in their practice. But in order to continue in love and faith one must have understanding. Then love will not grow cold in the presence of ingratitude nor faith wax dim before appearances of failure.

The next six lessons of this Primary Course deal with the special application of Truth to healing people of their beliefs in the reality of physical diseases and bodily weaknesses and limitations.

There may be said to be three general methods of healing by speaking the word of Truth: (1) the Argumentative; (2) the Intuitive; (3) by Spiritual Perception.

1 The Argumentative Method is a kind of silent teaching by which false impressions and errors are erased from the mind (carnal) and correct ideas and true conclusions, which are already in the true Mind of the patient, are brought forward, uncovered, and made to manifest in place of the false beliefs formerly held, just as when one is reasoned with to bring him out of believing in a lie, or fearing an apparition, or resting under a mesmeric spell.

2 The Intuitive Method is used by those who realize the inner guide, their impressional nature, and listen to the Truth within themselves. By the

intuition the healer knows just what expressions of Truth will reach the case. He may use argument, but will not be confined to any set formula. He will know when he should talk upon the Truth aloud to the patient and when to keep still. He exercises spiritual tact, and yet uncovers error fearlessly. He feels with true sympathy the needs of the patient and gives the meat or the milk of the Word according to the receptivity of his hearer and his degree of unfoldment.

Whoever is faithful to his intuitions in his treatments is that servant described by Jesus, "faithful and wise . . . whom his Lord hath made ruler over his household, to give them meat in due season." To him is promised, if he only continues faithful, that he shall rule "over all his goods." Matt. .'4:45-47.

3 In the method of Spiritual Perception no argument is used and often no word is spoken, either silently or audibly. The healer simply knows and his knowing becomes manifest. There is a flash of realization or a deep, still consciousness, indescribable with words, that this one is now perfectly well and whole, and this \\-r\cognition is like a great light that instantly destroys the error, called the disease, and immediately the healing is done. This was the principal method used by Jesus Christ, although at times he argued (Matt. 15: 23-28), and needed to speak the word more than once in certain cases (Mark 8:23-25). He used many methods, according to the exigency, but the same Spirit was in all his healing.

Students begin with the argumentative method, and as they become one with the truths of the teaching, they learn to follow their own impressions as to what they should say and do for individual cases. And many a new practitioner in mental healing has a holy baptism of realization (the third method) with his very first patients, so that he heals instantly one after another. It is not experience that produces the ablest mental healers but faithfulness to Principle in the daily life and realization of the truths he speaks for another.

Truth is so powerful that many times just mechanically expressing it is sufficient, but each healer must endeavor to feel what he says. One statement felt with deep, warm conviction is worth more than a dozen statements that are not realized.

As a definite aid to beginners a regular course of treatment will be described in the following six lessons, each lesson dealing with a set of errors to be overcome when a patient goes gradually, day by day, from his negative state, called disease, to his positive state, perfect health. The course is a Creative Week of manifestation, six days of work, or unfoldment, and a seventh day of rest, or full realization.

As Naaman, the leper, was dipped seven times in the river Jordan and came healed; as the children of Israel compassed Jericho seven days before its walls fell ; as the child whom Elisha brought back to life is said to have sneezed seven times in coming to consciousness, so it has seemed an orderly procedure to give most cases a course of seven treatments to wash away the errors of mortality, to raze to the ground delusion's structures, and cast out the false claims of personal sense.

Time has nothing to do with the healing, some taking their steps quickly and being healed in a few days, others not letting go their false thinking for weeks, though steadily gaining in the meanwhile. Let us never say, "It takes time to accomplish the healing." It is not time but realization, both on the part of the healer and the patient.

The first realization that one who would "pass from death unto life" (John 5:24), from disease to wholeness, must have is the truth about our real parentage, our inheritance and our generation.

God is the one Creator, the source of all true Being, and Man, His child, is made in His image and likeness. Therefore we are Spirit, since God is Spirit, and our Father and Mother is God. Our one Parent is the Holy One, who is perfect life and health pure, loving, and all-wise.

Accepting this as the truth of our origin and parentage, then we must conclude that from our divine Parent we can inherit only health and goodness, and the claim that we have an earthly parentage and are inheriting diseases and sinful habits is but a passing dream and without true foundation. Henceforth we repudiate and deny all these appearances of an evil physical and mental heritage.

We are not flesh, nor are we the children of mortal man, subject to the false beliefs of an earthly ancestry. We deny the reality of the flesh and its laws, and take our stand that the spiritual Self only is the child of God. "They which are the children of the flesh, these are not the children of God." Rom. 9:8.

The real law of inheritance is "Good comes from Good." The child of God, the Good, inherits perfect and unchangeable health, strength, purity, and holiness.

All so-called laws of evil are the shadow of divine laws. When evil is acknowledged as a power and presence it seems to echo the spiritual law of inheritance, "Good comes from Good," with the delusion, "Evil comes from evil."

This false law is annulled through the knowledge of the truth that evil has no life or intelligence, no creator, and no place in Being. Disease cannot propagate itself. Sin has no real strength or power to increase. Weakness is a negative, and has no power to pass from one to another. Foolishness and mistakes have no law of reproduction or power of perpetuation. It is men's belief in these things as real and as having laws of their own that has caused them to have their seeming dominion. The whole baseless fabric can dissolve, and be made void by any child of God speaking the truth about it.

"All flesh is grass and all the goodliness thereof is as the flower of the field: the grass withereth, the flower fadeth : because the spirit of the Lord bloweth upon it!' "All nations before him are as nothing; and they are counted to him less than nothing, and vanity." Is. 40:6, 7, 17. "The spirit is that which makes alive; the flesh profits nothing." John 6:63 (Wilson's Emphatic Diaglot).

"Call no man your father upon the earth : for one is your Father, which is in heaven." Matt. 23:9. By these words Jesus instructs us to make the same claim of heavenly parentage that he does.

The fear of heredity is sometimes the only error that needs to be removed from a patient's mind in order to heal him. Then, with this one treatment, he is set free.

Many are they who can testify to their release from the bondage of some disease or sin which was said to be their lot because of earthly parentage through denying the reality of a fleshly father and mother.

Why should good, Christian people patient, loving characters suffer from inherited affliction? Why do they not accept the promise? Why do they live under the law of Moses, as we read it in Exodus, twentieth chapter, fifth verse? Do they hate God, or Good? No. Then why should they apply that text "visiting the iniquity of the fathers upon the children unto the third and fourth generation of them ///(// hate me" to themselves when they believe they love Good, and are trying to serve Good all they can ?

Even under the old dispensation the curse is removed, as it is written : "The word of the Lord came unto me again, saying, What mean ye, that ye use this proverb concerning the land of Israel, saying The fathers have eaten sour grapes, and the children's teeth are set on edge? As I live, saith the Lord God, ye shall not have occasion any more to use this proverb in Israel" Eze. 18:1-3.

The curse of the inheritance of evil is removed for evermore by the Christ within, who says, "I am the Son of God," and "All things whatsoever thou hast given me are of thee." John 17:7.

Your health is perfect and sure. Your life is the life of God, immortal. You inherit only strength and purity. Your body is spiritual, therefore not corrupt, or weak, or paralyzed. God gives you nothing but what is in His own Being.

Universal statements, denials, and affirmations must be particularized in some cases in order to be realized. This is especially true in self-treatment. Therefore the healer must be patient and faithful to the word of Truth, and not be discouraged if the walls of Jericho do not fall at the first blasts. "Let us not be weary in well doing : for in due season we shall reap, if we faint not." Gal. 6:9.

While denying the earthliness of our parentage, the Christ-born student will not fail to "honor his father and mother" but will love and respect the Spirit in them as he does the Spirit in all. They are the representatives of a great, office in God. So also are all other earthly claims of relationship. God in everyone is our relative. We are all one holy family, of whom God is the Life and true Being.

The family circle is for the purpose of forming a nucleus where love can center and pour forth into avenues lawful and useful. When the family fulfills its part, it is like the little fence built about a growing tree of love to keep it from being trampled on while unfolding. But our love should not be confined to those called ours ; we are not to love them less, but we increase our love towards all the rest of our Family, thereby fulfilling the demands of our Christ-nature which has no respect of persons, but sees the Divine in all, the ideal which every true lover sees in his beloved.

Universal Brotherhood is based upon the principle of One Life in all the nations, "one body and one Spirit, . . . one God and Father of all, who is above all, and through all, and in you all." Eph. 4:4, 6. With God there is no bias as to race or nation. The Truth destroys all the barriers, such as pride, hatred, and exclusiveness between you and all races and nations, and you recognize but one people, the spiritual race in the Kingdom of Heaven.

God is without beginning and without end. Therefore, Man, His image, is also without beginning and without end. Always you have been. You did not begin at the appearance called your birth in the flesh. Being immortal, your soul has existed throughout the ages, and will, forevermore. Pre-existence is not a new teaching; the Pharisees had it among their tenets, and many of the blessings and curses of this life they ascribed to the virtues and sins of a previous existence.

Pre-existence is a truth, but the suppositions which have been attached to it, such as re-incarnation, metempsychosis, and evolution are still open questions. Though they may be among the facts or relative truths of this realm of appearances, yet they are not true of God. Therefore, let us leave them in the theoretical department of our mentalities, or, at most, use them only as "provisional hypotheses," which we can drop as readily as we take them up. It is sufficient for us to deal with the present fleshly problem, finishing all ignorance and misery in the body which we have now, and in this present age.

Divine experiences go hand in hand with divine consciousness, and these we shall always have. But the experiences which are not in the Life of God have no place or real power in our manifesting. The belief that one is in disease and pain because of the sins of a previous life must be cancelled. Your life has evermore been in God, as it is now. Let no claim of an evil past delude you into sickness.

You are Self-causing, Self-existent Being like God, all that you are being the result of what you have thought, and every moment you are thinking that which is the cause of the next moment's manifestation. Remember your God-origin and you thereby profit by it.

Side by side with the understanding of the true law of our inheritance goes the understanding of the true law of our generation. God is the one creator, not earthly man or woman. Since you are not flesh, you are not created by laws of flesh. Here we face the race-error of mortal man, belief that he or she can create the error which has been called "the original sin," thinking that flesh can generate and conceive.

There is but one conception, the Immaculate Conception that manifestation in the conceiving of Jesus Christ, which is type of the true origin of every child. At every conception the Spirit of God moves upon the face of the deep. Each one is sent of God.

You are Spirit, eternally conceived of God and born of God not in time, but in eternity. You have always lived, and always will live; you were never born into materiality or time, and you will never die. Realization of this truth is that process spoken of in Scripture as being "born of the Spirit" (John 3).

You are the child of purity and holy love. The love of God knows no lustful desire. There is nothing that degrades or shames in divine generation. In God, no enjoyment is carnal. All enjoyment is of the Spirit, spiritual, and not until man ceases to believe in sensual passions and carnal appetites can he know the real ecstasy of the Spirit, of which these are but the shadow. To love these things or to hate them is error, to uphold or to condemn them arises from ignorance. The true attitude is to know these appetites as non-existent to your higher Self and powerless to him that is free from delusion. The soul's pleasure, the holy delights of Spirit, are all in all to you.

False beliefs in fleshly and sensual gratification must be erased from the mind before their symbolic diseases can disappear. Speak the truth concerning the real Man: "Your desires are Spiritual, not carnal. All sensation is of the Mind, of the Spirit, and you do not look to the flesh for gratification. You are satisfied in God. Your joy is in the Lord. You are holy, pure, sweet, and clean in all your thoughts. God is your Purity. God is your holy Love and you desire only God"

Before pure and holy words no corrupt, unclean disease can stay.

As you speak the truth concerning one sensual appetite, you will see that it applies to all. Drunkenness, smoking, morphine habit all these are but out-picturings of mental hunger and thirst, which are never satisfied, but continually increased by material, temporal appeasings.

Such hunger and thirst are but the shadows of those spiritual desires which in the divine Mind are receiving perpetual satisfaction. "Blessed are they which do hunger and thirst after righteousness : for they shall be filled." Matt. 5:6.

Feed the drunkard with right thoughts about his true Self and he will be so satisfied that no saloon can tempt him, and no liquor can longer have any charms. Never treat him as a drunkard, by upbraiding or finding fault, or with impatience or disrespect. Act always as though he were himself and address him as One who is all-powerful to overcome. Recognize only the Christ in him, then you can understand that "inasmuch as ye have done it unto one of the least of these my brethren, ye have done it unto me." Matt. 25:40.

By commencing with the thoughts and desires of the drunkard "the ax is laid unto the root of the tree." Matt. 3:10. The old method of working on the outside signing the pledge, avoiding the saloon, keeping the wine bottle out of sight, scolding, blaming, condemning, is like pulling off the leaves of the tree to destroy it.

The true method strikes right at the root, or cause, which is interior the thinking, the carnal mind. The desire must be overcome, then the work is finished. Working externally is working in the letter, working internally is working in the Spirit. The letter and the Spirit can be fulfilled together, and this is harmonious and easy salvation.

Let us continually remember that the personal man can do nothing of himself, but God is the One that overcomes. Let God work in you and with you, and let the personal step aside. So shall every appetite be redeemed, and what have been stumbling blocks in our life may be made stepping stones to heaven.

St. Augustine! well hast thou said,
That of our vices we can frame
A ladder, if we but tread
Beneath our feet each deed of shame.

Longfellow.

Daily consecrate yourself to God to be used in His service as a Christian mental healer. Let your soul often voice the words of Mary, "Behold the handmaid of the Lord ; be it unto me according to thy word." Luke 1:38. By taking this attitude of mind faithfully you will be preparing yourself, and the Spirit in you will be drawing to you just those to be healed by you.

When any ask you to give them treatment do not refuse on the ground that another can do the work better than yourself. Such an attitude would be untrue to Principle, and a denial of the Lord within yourself.

It is well to wait until you are asked, and in some cases there should be a very earnest desire before any treatment is given.

Never treat anyone against his or her will. The exceptions to this rule are cases of insanity or vice, where a perverted will is the first error to be corrected.

The faith that the patient should have is simply that of not taking any other remedies not dieting or doing any other thing for his health, nor looking to any other physician or healer while under this treatment.

It is not necessary for you always to be in the personal presence of the patient. There is no distance or space with Mind, and the word of Truth reaches those who are absent as to the flesh just as easily as those present. Jesus shows this in two instances: John, fourth chapter, forty-sixth to fifty-second verses, and Matthew, eighth chapter, fifth to thirteenth verses.

By studying Christ's methods we shall have explained to us many points that we have observed in a true practice.

A few general suggestions can be given to you as a healer, but no fixed rules, for no two cases are treated just alike, though the principles are always the same.

Usually take the patient alone, not allowing any that are skeptical or unsympathetic to the method to be present.

It is advisable not to touch the patient.

Do not diagnose the disease or talk about it as a reality. It is not even necessary that you know what the disease is.

Talk little to him at first. Give him the great principles of the teaching, but do not look for him to use the Word for himself until further instructed, and you see that self-work is required to complete the healing.

The following is a good order of proceeding in giving treatment. Remember, the speaking is all silent.

1 Consecrate yourself.

2 Mentally address the patient by name.

3 Apply yourself to reassure him mentally that there is nothing to fear.

4 Tell him the truth about God and himself.

5 Make such denials and affirmations as are appropriate to the case. In a six-day course of treatment the first day you deny the belief in an evil inheritance and the reality and power of sensual desires and carnal appetites, and you affirm the truth about the divine inheritance and the pure and holy origin and desires.

6 Close with invoking a benediction upon yourself, the patient, and your Word of Truth, thus, "So shall my word be that goeth forth out of my mouth : it shall not return unto me void, but it shall accomplish that which I please, and it shall prosper in the thing whereto I sent it." Is. 55:11.

LESSON VIII. FREEDOM FROM DELUSIONS AND DECEPTIONS.

THE laws of the Kingdom of Heaven are the true laws, and the only ones that govern us in reality. It is because of ignorance that men feel themselves under the limitations and control of evil influences and laws. The truth, that Good is the only real presence and power, sets man free from the deceptions of evil and the delusions of matter.

Universal statements of Truth are often too abstract to be grasped by the mind that is struggling for freedom. Therefore we need to be specific in dealing with the errors that appear to face the student daily in his journey out of ignorance into the realm of the true. For there seem to be beliefs in evil that are held to unconsciously until attention is called to them, and measures taken to undeceive the mind that has been so falsely trained.

The true Mind is not deceived by evil appearances nor deluded by material laws, but the claim-to-intelligence, called the "carnal mind," is the one in error which needs to be undeceived, and freed from delusions. It is saved from its own false imaginings by giving up its claim and letting the divine Mind be its thinking.

The race, starting with the erroneous premise that Man is fleshly and mortal, and that materiality is true substance, seems to have involved itself in a maze of false conclusions. From childhood humanity is taught to believe in the evil influences of climate, the likelihood of accidents, the contagion of diseases, the contamination of associates, the limitations of physical laws. Fears, anxieties, distrust of men and animals, dread of future punishment, preparations and provisions for sickness, death, and old age these have all been considered legitimate states of mind by deluded mortals, and such errors must not be entertained in the mind that desires to manifest perfect health in self and others. We do not need to seek out these false beliefs, but when they seem to present themselves let us be alert not to give them place and power by unconsciously assenting to them as lawful and true.

To mortal sense some errors, such as those called sins, are greater than others, and yet there is no rank in error if one judges it by results, for the mental physician who diagnoses mind often traces the source of the most aggravating and painful diseases to such common beliefs in evil as worriment and anxiety, distrust, fears, small gossip, impatience, and petty sensitiveness. By neglecting to correct these insignificant errors many an otherwise good man or woman seems slow in being healed, while some flagrant sinner comes quickly to health because he repents and completely renounces the sin that lies back of his disease.

A slight mistake at the beginning of the solution of a problem may cause the answer to be far from true.

"Whatsoever is not of faith is sin" (Rom. 14:23), and the trifling admissions of the presence and power of evil are "the little foxes that spoil the vines." S. of S. 2:15. These must be eradicated utterly, for they have no part in the Divine Presence. The woman who frets, either secretly or openly, has no abiding place in the Kingdom of Heaven, but has all she can do to drive away headaches and dyspepsia, the natural outcome of her states of mind. The man who is filled with doubts and distrust concerning his fellowmen, or indulges either silently or aloud in sarcasm and criticism, cannot rest in the realm of heavenly peace he must look after his rheumatism. Only the one who faithfully holds to the power and law of the Good can remain in perpetual happiness.

The government of God is universal and omnipotent. Its laws are altogether spiritual and good. The true Man governs all things by the power of Mind, and being the image of God is subject to nothing but God, or Good.

The Child of the Most High is not influenced by the opinions of people or the advice of false counselors. He reflects only that which is highest and best in all mentalities. In your true Being you never "take on" diseases or become subject to contagion. "He shall deliver thee from the noisome pestilence. . . . There shall no evil befall thee, neither shall any plague come nigh thy dwelling." Ps. 91:3, 10. While yet you seem in closest contact with associates who are unregenerate, you can remain wholly free from every taint. If your loved ones are meeting companions whose influences seem hurtful remember the power of your silent Word to cause their true Self to be dominant, so that their goodness manifests many times more influence than all the vices of the others. In the divine economy positive virtue is continually brought in touch with negative characters to purify and vivify their mental atmospheres, and give them opportunity for reformation.

No one can be moved by the false in others except those who are not positive by reason of a knowledge of the Truth, and those who believe in the power of an evil mind.

The error that is at the root of hypnotic practice is the believing in more than one mind, and that one mind can impose an untruth upon the mind of another.

True mental practice never breathes a statement that is a falsehood, or suggests a state of being or an action unworthy of God.

Truth heals by de-hypnotizing the patient, thus freeing him from the mesmerisms of mortal sense.

The Truth student who is true to his principles never hypnotizes anyone, but speaks what he devoutly believes to be true of the God-Man, and so, as it were, awakens the patient to true consciousness not depriving him of self - consciousness as is done in ordinary hypnosis.

If we do not deceive ourselves by our own personal desires or fears of evil we cannot fall under the hypnotic spell of another. Never hypnotize others, and so keep yourself exempt from all its claims to influence. For, truly, hypnotism has no real power all its apparent control comes through some one's belief in it, not always under its modern name, but under such terms as fascination, charm, bewitchery, etc. It is the shadow-side of divine influence, and is now on its way out of superstition into science, to be lifted up and wholly redeemed through humanity ceasing to be swayed by its fears and passions.

The Law of God sets you free from every evil influence, and you realize that there is really no power in evil association for anyone. God, the Good, is the One Influence in all and through all. You cannot be contaminated by any evil at all. Though in the world you do not partake of the world. Instead of being affected by evil influences, you are the salt of the earth, and all are salted by God in you, and made to feel clean, and pure, and healthy by your very presence, even if you do not say a word.

Meet all the malpractice of those who use their minds against you with fearless love-thoughts, and turn every curse into a blessing. "No weapon that is formed against thee shall prosper." Is. 54:17. "Thou shalt be hid from the scourge of the tongue : neither shalt thou be afraid of destruction when it cometh." Job 5 12 1. No poisonous thought can affect those who meet all malice with the antidote of love.

One, only, has any right to control you God. No human will should be allowed to usurp the throne of your mind, whether it claims to be in the flesh or out of it. Mediumship and hypnotism have the same mistaken basis, and their effects upon their victims are the best arguments against their false rule. Our divine birthright is Individuality, which may be manifest in the flesh by our being true to our God, and by acknowledging His right only to control us, and govern our minds and actions.

Those who practice with Truth grow clearer in mind, purer in character, healthier and stronger in body the more they use it, and live by it. They do not grow exhausted in their healing power, but gain continually by giving. By this the true practice may be known.

The laws of health are Spiritual, not material, and they cannot be broken, for they are of God. Whoever abides by them will never know any limitation to his strength in doing good, nor lose his health or life while in unselfish service for others. The first law of health in which your consciousness must be well rooted is: God is your health, and the source and cause of your health. Your health and strength do not depend upon what you eat, neither can they be affected by anything you eat. Man does not live by material bread, but Man lives by the Word of God. To realize that the Thoughts of God and not material things feed us is to find ourselves freed from anxiety about eating and drinking. It is not what we eat that poisons the blood or weakens the system, but our thoughts of evil. "There is nothing from without a man, that entering into him can defile him: but the things which come out of him, those are they that defile the man" (Mark 7:15), said Jesus, and when his disciples asked him to explain, he told them plainly the sources of corruption, whether physical or mental :

"And he said, That which cometh out of the man, that defileth the man. For from within, out of the heart of men, proceed evil thoughts, adulteries, fornications, murders, thefts, covetousness, wickedness, deceit, lasciviousness, an evil eye, blasphemy, pride, foolishness: all these evil things come from within, and defile the man." Mark 7:20-23.

Eating and drinking represent mental appropriation of ideas, and what we eat and drink symbolizes the kind of thoughts we are taking. Eat and drink of the words of Christ, Truth, and nothing can hurt you. Eat the divine Word and you will never starve.

Make no laws for yourself as to what you shall eat and what you shall drink, or as to how you shall dress, or about bathing, or exercise, or any of those things that the worldly physician thinks are the all-important factors of right living.

No great master of life has ever given any physiological laws to the world. No such law is fixed and certain, or of universal application. To the contrary, they who endeavor to make so-called laws of health agree that "one man's meat is another man's poison" that is, what is good law for one man will kill another.

Instead of giving laws concerning the external treatment of the body, the great Master, Jesus Christ, says, "Therefore take no thought, saying, What shall we eat or what shall we drink or wherewithal shall we be clothed?" Matt. 6:31. This is the advice of one who knew all about right living.

"Eat such things as are set before you" (Luke 10:8), he says to his disciples. "And these signs shall follow them that believe, ... if they drink any deadly thing it shall not hurt them." Mark 16:17, 18. "Nothing shall by any means hurt you." Luke 10:19. This is because "your names are written in heaven"

(Luke 10:20) that is, you realize your being and character (name) is established and under the law (written in) of the spiritual kingdom (Heaven).

You are Spirit, governed by the law of Spirit, and no earthly thing can affect you. You cannot be fatigued by material things. "They that wait upon the Lord . . . shall run and not be weary; and they shall walk, and not faint." Is. 40:31.

Whoever believes himself to be Spirit, and that matter is unreal, will not test the Truth ("tempt the Lord") by such thinking and acting as, "I will put my hand in the fire and see if God will keep it from burning." Such words come not from trust in God and realization that no earthly element can destroy Man, but from doubt of God, and assumption of the possibility of materiality to harm one. You are not tempting God when you go forward about your "Father's business" of doing good, fearless of every material law and evil condition. You cannot be overworked in doing good, or be in danger from pestilence or evil men when abroad upon an errand for Christ.

You live in the spiritual world where nothing can hurt you or injure you ; water cannot drown you, nor fire burn you, nor the air bring you disease, pestilence, "colds" impurities, and so forth ; where the weather is never too warm or too cold, and the climate is ever healthy. Let us cease talking about the evils of the weather and the dangers from the elements, "for our conversation is in heaven" (Phil. 3:20), and "for every idle word that men shall speak they shall give account." Matt. 12:36. Speak the word for others, as well as for yourself, that these things cannot harm them. Mentally deny their fears and prognostications of calamity.

God is our defense is the understanding that brings deliverance from all disasters and accidents, and protects the lover of Good from all enmity, whether among animate or inanimate things. By this knowledge Daniel was protected from the lions, the "three children" delivered from the flames, and

LESSON IX. FORGIVENESS, THE CURE OF SIN.

EYEN a slight knowledge of God's Truth has healed case after case through removing fear and restoring confidence in life and health as greater powers than disease and death.

Many a captive has been set free from the bonds of sickness and sorrow, misery and poverty, just through the realization that these things are subject to mind and that they are not necessary evils, since they have no part or place in the true Life.

To begin to be conscious of our freedom from the law of an evil and fleshly inheritance (Lesson 7), and that we are not in bondage to the laws of physical causation (Lesson 8), is sufficient to cast off multitudes of the ills to which flesh seems to be heir, and day after day the student sees himself released from daily afflictions and annoyances. He does not catch cold now through fears of draft or damp, knowing that he is Spirit, and cannot be affected by material changes. He does not suffer from indigestion, for he has ceased to give power to his food. He no longer thinks he must have heart disease or consumption, cancer or rheumatism, because his earthly parents suffered from it. Many evils vanish from his life through the very first shining of the rays of knowledge. With the prophet he has learned, "My people are destroyed for lack of knowledge" (Hos. 4:6), and that even a superficial knowledge has great restoring power in it.

But there are some conditions which do not seem to yield so readily as others conditions which are called chronic, and these, we must know, leave only upon the erasure of sin, or some secret belief in evil called sin, by the one who is showing forth the inharmonious, chronic condition.

Most chronic cases are caused by belief in sin on some one's part; they are the out-picturing of a belief in sinning or in being sinned against, usually both.

"Why do good people so often suffer with chronic diseases?" will naturally be asked. It is true they seem to be perfect in character, but ask them whether they are without sin and they will tell you they are far from sinless no matter how peaceful they may seem externally, there is often a fierce battle raging within. An accusing conscience lies at the root of their disease, and not until they stop condemning themselves can they be free from the law of condemnation, which is always delivering the accused to the judge,, who delivers to the officer, who casts into prison (Matt. 5:25).

As mortals we cannot say we are without sin. "If we say we have no sin, we deceive ourselves" (I John 1:8), as even Paul says, "For I know that in me (that is, in my flesh) dwelleth no good thing" Rom. 7:18.

It is only as the Son of the Most High, God's image, that we can say, "I am holy, sanctified, perfect as my Heavenly Father, and cannot sin."

Good men and women are suffering because, while they are doing good outwardly, they have not been able to do good within. They are fulfilling the letter of the moral law, but not its spirit.

Not only must a man put away evil from his acts and words, but also he must put it away from his thoughts. The invalid who, while calm and patient outwardly, is attacked in thought with impatience and bitterness must learn a law by which he can control his thoughts, and be as serene and kind within as he is without, and then shall his "health spring forth speedily." The man who "cannot forget," even while he claims to forgive, is not on the road that leads to immortal health.

Jesus came to a religious nation which was most punctilious in fulfilling the letter of the Mosaic law, but its people's thoughts were not in Truth. Few of them had realized the power of their minds, therefore they needed One who was in active knowledge and demonstration of the power of thinking to show them how to live so as to bring to pass the results of wholehearted obedience to the laws which they had received from Moses and the prophets.

In the Sermon on the Mount Jesus shows that a man must cease to kill in mind as well as in deed, that he must be chaste in thought as well as outwardly, that he must not steal mentally, such as envy and covetousness, nor return evil for good even in thought. The good people of to-day who are in pain and trouble and want are learning to take these experiences as signs that something is wrong. They cry, "I do not steal, I do not lie, I do not commit adultery, I do by my neighbor as I would be done by. Why is it, then, that I am so afflicted?" And again the Truth is sounding, "Except your righteousness shall exceed the righteousness of the scribes and Pharisees, ye shall in no case enter into the kingdom of heaven." Matt. 5:20.

Let us consider some of the directions for right living which Jesus gave in the Great Discourse. He says, "Ye have heard that it was said by them of old time, Thou shalt not kill, and whosoever shall kill shall be in danger of the judgment: but I say unto you, That whosoever is angry with his brother is in danger of the judgment" Matt. 5:21, 22. That is, not only must a man refrain from killing with his hands and his words, but also he must refrain from all angry thinking. Are you impatient? Must you continually suppress anger? Do you allow your temper to foam and ferment within ? Where do you think such force goes ? It is plain to be seen how the character and circulation of the blood is influenced by angry thinking how the face pales or flushes under such emotion. And when it is considered how blood is becoming tissue and fibre of organs, muscles, and bones one can readily see how angry blood makes angry organs, muscles, and bones, which then show forth tumors, cancers, and irritating and inflamed diseases of all kinds. This is the judgment of which we are in danger.

Our judgment is not put off until some future Day of Judgment. Every day the false thoughts are being separated from the true, the false joining the conditions of evil, torment, pain, disease, and so forth, and the true entering into the rest of their Lord, the Good. If we let our consciousness be identified with the untrue, then it will seem to be ourselves that are tormented, and suffer with pain and sorrow. We cannot be angry at all, else we come under the old law of Moses, which condemns and punishes.

God is Love, and in Him is no anger at all. You, as the child of God, are the image of pure, changeless Love, and in your true nature no evil temper can abide. We delude ourselves if we ever justify anger in ourselves or in others. It rises from a belief in the reality of evil and from believing in our impotency to cope with it. Trueness to our principle, "Good is the only real power," will strike right at the root of every false emotion, and heal us forever of all anger.

In so far that you do not speak angry words, or commit angry deeds, well and good. This is fulfilling the letter of the law, and now you are ready to fulfill the spirit of the law by not thinking angry thoughts.

To put away from us all angry thinking is to put out all malice, revenge, resentment, impatience, hatred, spitefulness, and all the murderous brood forever. Watch your thoughts continuously, and let only the Christ-love reign in your heart and mind. To every angry thought say, "I know you not," or "You are not of me" or "No," or "There is no evil," or "It is nothing" some form of true denial which "prepares the way of the Lord" and thus gets the mind ready to entertain the true thought, the Christ "Love is all," "Peace," "Almighty Good reigns," affirmations of the true.

The Spirit will inspire you with some word or sentence to which you can always resort the instant the temper begins to rise. One student was healed by using the sentence, "Love is patient and kind ;" another found great help in "All is Good ;" a third would watch her breath and heart and say, "Peace! be still," over and over until unmoved.

Also the word of Truth must be spoken for your neighbor that needs to be redeemed from angry passions. In order that you may be wholly forgiven (be given the Christ-thought in place of evil-thinking) you must forgive others, which is, to give them the Christ-thought in place of evil-thinking. Has some one you know an evil temper ? Does some one continually scold, and fret, and find fault? Tell him the Truth about himself tell it mentally : "You are the child of Love, and Love rules your every thought. You are, in your real Self, gentle and loving, patient and kind. God is your. peace. Christ reigns in your heart. You love to be kind and gentle. God bless you." "Give people this bread of life at all times, and never withhold your hand. God shows you how to forgive, for it is God in you who is really forgiving.

Many people are healed of old, chronic diseases just by getting rid of their tempers, or some old, secret, revengefulness or resentment, or some poisonous hatred.

The next commandment Jesus refers to is, "Thou shalt not commit adultery." He then proceeds to show that lustful thoughts must be rooted out of the heart in order that one be free from adulterous consequences disease in the body and disorder in affairs.

Our thinking must be pure and holy. "Ye shall be holy, for I am holy." Lev. 11:144. To cleanse the mind of impure thoughts realize that they are not yours, that they are not real, that they are nothing. The only One who thinks in us is God, and God is pure, and thoughts which He does not have are vanity and nothingness. Do not fight them. Do not condemn yourself or another for them. But continually think, "Christ thinks in me now I am pure, I am holy, I am clean. God is the only presence in my heart."

If others seem to be possessed by impure thinking, speak the same words for them. Do not feel that you can be contaminated by their presence. Jesus Christ touched the lepers, contrary to the Hebrew law, and he was not harmed, whereas they were cleansed. Do not condemn. Remember Jesus' words to the adulteress, "Neither do I condemn thee: go, and sin no more." John 8:11. This is "casting out devils." A man may be so possessed of a false idea that he seems the walking personification of that idea, and so misers, fanatics, people "out of their mind," are said to be obsessed, or possessed of devils. The healing of such is through the healer realizing that there is but one idea to be possessed of, and that is the Christ. See everyone as pure in God. See the holy One in all. Do not dwell upon the actions and speech of the personality, but think of the pure One. "Blessed are the pure in heart, for they shall see God." Matt. 5:8.

"Ye have heard that it hath been said, An eye for an eye, and a tooth for a tooth: but I say unto you, That ye resist not evil." Matt. 5:38, 39. Evil has never been destroyed by meeting it with evil. Good is the only power that can annihilate evil. As long as we are sensitive to evil, and recognize it as a power, it will seem to come into our lives. By meeting the hand that is raised to strike you with loving, fearless knowledge that you cannot be injured, and your assailant does not really wish to hurt you, the threatening hand cannot touch you. By meeting the arrows of sarcasm and criticism with active love-thoughts, even though not a word is spoken by you, the unkind remarks will fall flat and stingless. Deny all sense of injury, imposition, and wrong which you may seem to have, and look faithfully for the false appearances to be taken out of your life. They may seem to remain as long as you can feel them evil ; the instant you cease to care about them, they will seem, almost miraculously, to fade out of your life.

Love your enemies (Matt. 5 144) by seeking for God, who is your friend, in them. Meet them in soul, and realize that in Spirit each understands and loves the other. Personal actions and evil ways do not count, and cannot deceive you. Convert all your enemies into friends by steadfastly remembering their divine Sonship, and what they are to God, who is their life and power to be, as well as yours.

"Judge not, that ye be not judged." Matt. 7:1. Do not talk about the evil in others. Do not call attention to the evils in another. The word of the Christ is. "I judge no man." John 8:15. Your word is, "I judge no man."

Have that love for all that sees no faults. If you would not speak about the faults of your best beloved, then do not speak of the faults of any. It is said, "Love is blind," because love sees no evil in the loved one. Love has the true sight, for it sees only the Good. "Love thinketh no evil." 1 Cor. 13:5. You are one with love in thinking no evil.

The one head under which all false beliefs called sins are said to come is "selfishness." And the error of selfishness arises from thinking there is another self besides God. "Hear, O Israel, the Lord our God is one Lord. Mark 12:29. There is only one Self God. And God owns all this, nothing can be taken from Him. There is no stealing from God. All happiness, all possessions, are His, therefore yours, you being in Him. There is no envy with God, no covetousness, for all is His. To be desirous of the world's goods, which are vanity, is the error called "covetousness."

God gives freely of His love and His honors and His glory. There is no jealousy with God. He who is afraid of losing his rightful share of love, or his rightful praise, is in the error of jealousy and a false self-love. Let him learn that the love that changes is not real, nor the praise that is misplaced lasting. He is truly healed of jealousy as he realizes that love given to another does not lessen his share, and praise given to another does not take from him. There is only One who is glorified in all expression of appreciation the great Life and Spirit of us all.

Ignorance is the cause of sinning. In the Bible the word "sin" means "missing the mark" a term applied to an archer whose arrow has failed in its flight. We are all aiming at the mark Happiness, and whoever is not attaining eternal happiness is "missing the mark." All sin is ignorance. Ignorance of what is sin ? No ; not ignorance of what is evil or sin. The veriest savage has his ideas of a right and a wrong, and holds something as a sin for which there should be a punishing. The ignorance is the false idea of what will bring happiness or, at least, satisfaction.

The murderer thinks it is to his satisfaction to kill. He soon proves how ignorant he has been through the sufferings, either within or without, that he has brought upon himself. The embezzler sees no way out of some dilemma but to steal. Here is ignorance of the fact that God is his salvation, and that faithfulness to Principle, God, can lift him out of any trouble, no matter how complicated.

The only way to set the sinner free is to dissolve him in each one by the pure words of Truth, declaring the unreality of the sinner and the sin, and the reality of the sinless one, the Son of God. This is done by the mind putting away from the human heart and recognition all thought of committing sin, all accusing others of sin, and all meditation upon sin as a real presence and power.

The divine gift of dissolving sinful desires and intents of the heart, and destroying their consequences (misery in body, mind, and circumstances), is called in the Gospel, "the forgiveness of sin." This God-power is now vested in you as the manifestation of God in the flesh, called the "Son of man" in the Scriptures. "That ye may know that the Son of man hath power on earth to forgive sins" (Matt. 9:6) Jesus proved by freeing a man whom sin had bound with palsy. "For the Father judgeth no man, but hath committed all judgment unto the Son . . . and hath given him authority to execute judgment also, because he is the Son of man." John 5:22, 27.

For every error, mistake, sin, which comes to any of our senses we are to give the Truth, that is, just the opposite. The derivation of the word "forgive," "to give for," will serve to keep one in mind of its original power. It substitutes for a sin the opposite virtue. Thus to forgive adultery in others is to cleanse them of adulterous desires and call forth the purity in them; to forgive hate is to cause love to spring up in its place.

True forgiveness is just as substantial an act as the giving of money is said to be, and as God works through man to carry out His benevolent designs towards the weak and poor, so He erases sin by working through the mind of man to send healing, loving thoughts towards those who seem in the delusion of sinful, unwholesome minds and lives.

We are not only to forgive (1) those who sin against us personally, but also (2) those who sin against our beloved, and (3) those who sin against the lovable and innocent anywhere upon the earth.

There must be no limit to our forgiveness. Some errors seem so deeply rooted that it requires angelic patience and deific persistency in order to eradicate them. Therefore when Peter asked Jesus how often he should forgive his brother "till seven times? Jesus saith unto him, I say not unto thee, Until seven times : but, Until seventy times seven." Matt. 18:21, 22.

True forgiveness cleanses and sanctifies those who are receptive to it. And the out-picturing of this divine process is in being cleansed of the corrupting disease which was caused by the sin, and in having purer, holier motives and thoughts.

"Forgive us our debts, as we forgive our debtors." Matt. 6 :12. "If ye do not forgive, neither will your Father which is in heaven forgive your trespasses." Mark 11:26. As you give to others true, righteous thoughts and see them good, spiritual, and lovable, you will make yourself receptive to the same thoughts that are ever radiating from the Father's presence. God does not cease to forgive; it is wayward man that ceases to receive. We must be receptive to the Divine Presence, else it will not seem to exist for us.

If you wish to be forgiven a certain vice, you must silently and faithfully speak the word that sets others free from that same vice. It is God in you the Good, Truth, in you that is the forgiving power.

As long as one believes in sin, so long will he believe in punishment for sin, and no one can escape the effect of sin, suffering, but by the putting away from him of all sinful thinking, speaking, and doing.

If we believe another ought to be punished for sin, that punishment is as likely to come to us as to the other, although we may not consider ourselves as deserving of punishment. So the only true attitude of mind is to be glad and willing to see everyone set free from punishment, and to be an instrument in the divine hands for the consummation of this great work by being glad and willing to give the Truth to all who will receive it in place of the error which they seem to be holding. For the only freedom from punishment is in knowing the Truth.

Men and women who are leading sinful lives and are not suffering for it are free thus far because they have not yet come under their own condemnation, nor care for the condemnation of others. There will come a time when they will desire to rise above their present limitations some one will come into their lives whose love and respect they will begin to desire then there must be a change, and, alas ! for them, if perversity and unbelief, because of much iniquity, will cause them to be long in accepting the Truth that will make them free.

People who are suffering keenly are often nearer the Truth than those who are content with selfish, impure living. And those are not the greatest sinners who have the most diseases. No one knows established health but the sinless One. "Those eighteen, upon whom the tower in Siloam fell, and slew them, think ye that they were sinners above all men that dwelt in Jerusalem? I tell you, Nay: but, except ye repent, ye shall all likewise perish." Luke 13:4, 5.

Pity and indignation at the manifestation of a wrong are strong powers which must be turned to usefulness in thwarting the injurious effects that seem imminent. These two forces have their source in the sense of love and justice, and therefore should be used to accomplish these ends. If you see an animal receiving cruel blows, instead of letting your pity be wasted in a feeling of impotence and misery, send your love in warm, living currents to the Life in the creature, declaring : "Your life is the life of God, protected and kept from all harm. No blows can hurt you. Good is the only power in you and around you ;" and to the master say : "The wisdom and love of God work through you to bring forth the Good you wish" or words of like nature. Your word will take away all the sting from the lash, and bring the inflictor to true consciousness.

If you see a widow being defrauded by a dishonest money-grabber, do not let your indignation be wasted in anger and powerless denunciation. You may be mistaken in your judgment of the whole affair. Instead of dwelling upon the evil of the situation, say to him: "You desire only Good, and in your true Self you work for her highest Good as well as yours, and find your joy in it," and to her you say : "Everything he does is a blessing, a help, and an advantage to you ; God protects you," and your word shall not return to you void.

Wherever there appears to be a sinner or one sinned against, there is your opportunity for the exercise of your divinely ordained task of forgiveness through Almighty Love.

Proceed with your patient as in the two previous treatments, with the exception of the fifth step, which upon this day is the denial of the power of sin and affirmation of the omnipotence of Love.

Intuition will reveal to you what particular belief in sin you are to dissolve with the word of Truth ; but if you are not yet cognizant of this impressional nature, then you can about cover the ground by denying the reality and power of selfishness, pride, avarice, envy, jealousy, and malice.

One method of treatment is that of continually realizing the Divine Character and Man's unity with It.

Remember, it is what you realize that counts. Avoid superfluity of words and vain repetition. Feel the Truth of what you say.

SELF-TREATMENT.

God is Love. I am the child of Love, and, like my Father, all-loving and forgiving.

God is my loving patience ; no anger can control me.

God is my meekness ; pride has no place in me.

God is my forgiving spirit ; I cannot hold malice or revenge in my heart.

I am one with God, and possess all things ; therefore I covet nothing.

Like God, I freely give all things to all ; I know no selfishness.

I am filled with love ; I breathe love ; I radiate love.

I receive love from all, and no sinful thought can touch me. I cannot be moved by another's anger or pride. No one's selfishness, revenge, avarice, envy, or jealousy can affect me, or cause me to suffer; therefore I am free from all disease and sickness.

I now lovingly, fearlessly, and freely forgive all my fellowmen all sins committed against me and against the world, and I thank my Heavenly

Father that I am now fully forgiven, and I henceforth manifest perfect life, strength, and health forever. Amen.

LESSON X. OVERCOMING FEAR.

SALVATION consists in being saved from sinning and from its results sickness, sorrow, and death. There is no escape from the exact consequences of sinful deeds and thoughts but through the knowledge of Truth, by which comes the forgiveness which destroys sin and all its unhappy fruits.

The highest God-knowledge and power is needful sometimes to make restitution and reparation to others whom we have sinned against, and with mortals it would seem impossible, but to the Divine within you all things are possible.

The Mosaic law was a revelation to the Hebrews of moral causes and their physical effects. "Whatsoever a man soweth that shall he also reap" (Gal. 67) is the tenor of the whole Levitical law. To Cain it was revealed that he who kills will be killed again and again ("Everyone that findeth me shall slay me" Gen. 4:14) unless placed under the protection of the Lord, as it is written, "Therefore whosoever slayeth Cain, vengeance shall be taken on him sevenfold." Gen. 4:15. He who defrauds and cheats will suffer loss either in this age or in some other. He who deceives will be deceived. He who slanders will, in his turn, be bitten it may not be by a slander but by a scourging, physical disease.

Divine metaphysics prove the logic and law back of the Golden Rule "All things whatsoever ye would that men should do to you, do ye even so to them: for this is the law and the prophets." Matt. 7:12. For if we are not under the law of the Christ every word and deed will bring forth after its kind, and as it is with plants, the fruits will often far exceed the small seeds sown. "It is easier for heaven and earth to pass, than one tittle of the law to fail." Luke 16:17. But if we have the simplest knowledge of the Christ-truth, then can the heavens and the earth (the old conceptions) be rolled together like a scroll, and be clean dissolved to our consciousness, and we live in the new heavens and the new earth, exempt from the karmic laws of good for good and evil for evil.

Fate, destiny, astrological laws, and karma are all under the control of him who knows his Christhood. "Though his sins be as scarlet, they shall be as white as snow" (Is. 1:18), and not one seed need to bring forth an evil harvest, but "every plant, which my heavenly Father hath not planted, shall be rooted up." Matt. 15:13.

When one has thoroughly repented of an error and turned from it, he should let it pass completely out of mind. Continued remorse is contrary to the principle, "Only the Good is true." Regrets and sorrows over the past must be banished wholly from consciousness. "Thou shalt forget thy misery, and remember it as waters that pass away." Job 11:16.

The memory is renewed and revived by righteous forgetting forgetting the evils and the nothings, the vanities of existence, and remembering only its eternal verities, the Good and the Divine.

True repentance is our flight from some burning Sodom and Gomorrah, and when we have once left an evil state let us not look back upon it. "Remember Lot's wife." Luke 17:32. Those who dwell in past experiences grow fossilized, and age early. There is only the eternal present, the Now-Good, for us to live in. Whatever joys and happiness we have had in the past belong to the Kingdom of Heaven, and we shall know them again, for they are eternal.

Even though we appear to fall into sin again and again, yet each time we should rise up as though we had not fallen. No one is beaten unless he thinks he is. There is no backsliding in Truth. If a person seems to fall away, then you may know that one was not as advanced as appearances indicated. Never think you have "gone back" from Truth. You may seem to be in the valley many days, not seeing the Way as plainly as when you were on the mountain-tops, yet you are nearer your goal. While you are going through extreme experiences you are in mountainous regions of mind, and progression will be marked by many ups and downs, going into valleys as well as ascending mountain peaks. The spokes of a wheel cannot always remain up if the wheel is to go forward. They go down before they come up again, and when they are down they are further along than when up before.

Onward and upward is the law of the Good in the realm of growth and change, and the Truth follower is ever progressing, never really going backward but for the purpose of gathering force to go forward.

As leaven or yeast works in the midst of flour so the Word of Truth works among the thoughts and desires of man, a kind of mental, chemical action setting in wherein there seems to be disturbance and disorder, but to the eyes of the one who knows, a most desirable state preparatory to a new and useful manifestation. In many cases the "working" is deep and quiet, and where there is quick healing or realization of Truth, there is a momentary thrill or a strange, pleasant feeling not easy to describe. Every atom of the being is readjusted and bears new relation to every other atom. While this adjusting is going on one needs to be firm and true to Principle, that the work of casting out false beliefs may be thoroughly accomplished, and the birth into the new consciousness be quick and free from useless experiences.

When liquor is fermenting many foreign things are thrown to the surface which are then easily skimmed off. So the leaven of the Word will seem to bring hidden errors to the surface, and instead of being alarmed if a character seems to be worse after the Truth has begun its work, or a case of healing shows sudden and unusual symptoms of pain or change, the student must recognize this stage that comes between the old and the new, and carry the case quickly past its crisis into perfect relief and cure.

This stage has been described as the warring between Truth and error, the latter being slow to give up its claim, and possessed with fear of losing its life and being, so that the patient thinks himself to be in danger, and afraid of unknown consequences. Therefore fear is the principal error to be met at this time, and not another step is to be taken until fear is eliminated from the mind.

Often a denial of evil will seem to make the evil more real to one's self, but if the student will persist, denying the specific forms of evil that keep coming to the surface, soon the crisis will be passed, and he will come into a new and beautiful consciousness of Truth which was formerly hidden by the fogs of his erroneous belief.

If, when denying matter, new and unusual experiences begin to come, then deny fear calmly and slowly, and when the fear is brushed aside old material chains will also fall, and the omnipotence and omnipresence of Mind be more of a reality than ever.

The Word is like a broom sweeping our house (the body) and often a great dust is raised in the process. Uninstructed minds often stop, through fear, when their work is only partly done. But he who trusts in Life, in Health, in Good, will press right on to the finish, knowing that "in due season we shall reap if we faint not." Gal. 6:9.

Every error must be uncovered and its secret claims met fearlessly by the very name that mortals have given it, and be proven without place, power, or intelligence. To mention a secret belief in the presence of one who realizes its nothingness is sufficient to erase the whole thing from mind. This is the reason why the heart desires to confess to one in whom it has confidence, and feels such relief in confessing. Whenever you feel that you must tell your troubles to some one, select some strong, loving mentality who will make nothing of the evils you tell, and your wisdom will be rewarded with a perfect unburdening and sense of freedom peculiar to candor and innocence. Then you will know the reason of the advice, "Confess your faults one to another, and pray one for another, that ye may be healed." Jas. 5:16.

As a healer many sins and sorrows may be told you that have never been breathed to any one. But you should never whisper such confidences to another. The honor that governs the priest and the doctor should be yours.

And more than this, you would be untrue to your principles were you to repeat the tales of evil that are poured into your ears. Forget them as quickly as possible, or if they remain in your memory, let them be a suggestion to silently breathe a blessing to the one who has confessed, couching the blessing in words especially appropriate for their realization of the complete absolving of the wrong doing.

God is Love, inspiring fullness of confidence in His goodness, and bringing unlimited trust in His perfect protection and defense. There is no fear in the Divine Presence. Fear is carnal and has no place in the spiritual nature. "Perfect love casteth out fear; because fear hath torment. He that feareth is not made perfect in love." 1 John 4:18. There is no fear in love, and if we seem to have the slightest fear remaining, whether of God or man, beast or devil, we may know there is a vacuum in us demanding the in-filling of divine Love.

"The fear of the Lord," spoken of in Proverbs, ninth chapter, tenth verse, means reverence for the Lord, without which there cannot be either divine Wisdom or divine Love. Perfect love of God reveals to us that we have absolutely nothing to fear from the Author of All-goodness, in whom there is no evil thing, and that we can trust to His presence and power in everything that lives and has being. "For God hath not given us the spirit of fear ; but of power and of love and of a sound mind." 2 Tim. 1:7.

The fearful are classified with murderers and liars in Revelations, twenty-first chapter, eighth verse, as having no part in the realm of the True, but as being destined to pass through purging fires, that the false may be consumed, and all that is worth anything may be refined and set free from its tormenting presence. Therefore there is no justification for retaining fear of anything or anybody, and every student should be in training to cast out every fear from his being through the power of Trust and Almighty Love.

"Put on the whole armor of God" (Eph. 6:11), and realize the promises extended to all who are fearless because of complete trust in omnipotent Good. A large percentage of diseases rise from fears, either conscious or latent. Especially is this manifest among children, who are often thoughtlessly frightened with hobgoblin stories, and untrue threats of harm, and cruel tricks of the ignorant parents who little know that they are sowing the seeds of the disease that may bereave their household. Every child should learn the protecting presence of God to keep it from all injury and harm.

"He shall deliver thee in six troubles: yea, in seven there shall no evil touch thee. In famine he shall redeem thee from death: and in war from the power of the sword. Thou shalt be hid from the scourge of the tongue: neither shalt thou be afraid of destruction when it cometh. At destruction and famine thou shalt laugh: neither shalt thou be afraid of the beasts of the earth. For thou shalt be in league with the stones of the field: and the beasts of the field shall be at peace with thee." Job 5:19-23.

All the animal world is harmless before true love and fearlessness. Truth forms an aura of protection about its devotee more impenetrable than walls of stone. It is authentic history that many of the early Christians could not be made the prey of the hungry lions and tigers turned loose upon them, but some beasts would even go and lie down at the feet of those lovers of God like domestic animals to which the savage instinct is foreign. It was by this law that Daniel was delivered from the lions. The rattlesnake will never strike where there is freedom from both fear and harmfulness. "Blessed is the man who is afraid of nothing and of whom nothing is afraid."

If there is any animal -which you hate or fear, be it mouse, cat, dog, cow, snake, or any other, see to it that you purge your heart wholly from such feelings by the power of love which makes you one with the life of everything, and able to discern that Presence in them which the naturalist and the holy man find, and respect too highly to have a vain or foolish thought concerning.

Fear of people leaves us as we regard all as our brothers, and radiate to them the love that disarms their enmity. The thief could not then steal from you, nor the libertine insult you. Your life would be as safe with the savage as his very own. It would be as impossible for him to kill you as to cut off his own hand.

No domineering mentality can cause you to cower, nor wound you with tongue or any other weapon.

Fear of death, of the dark, of unknown powers and nameless things are all negations, or blanks, to be filled in with positive and definite expressions of trust and faith.

Every intimation of fear is a little flag of warning, telling us where our faith must be increased and strengthened, and we must never fear itself, but make use of its appearance to speak rousing, steadying words of the supremacy of Good.

When a patient is going from stage to stage, daily through a six days' course of treatment, he will grow better each day, receiving evidence continually of the power of the Word in healing him. After an effectual treatment against belief in sinning and being sinned against there follows a mental stage of activity comparable to the effervescence in a liquid wherein an acid and an alkali come together. The patient comes to judgment, mentally and physically, and there begins to be a casting out of false conditions and states of mind preparatory to entering the new, normal, and healthy state of body and of thinking. The commonest physical method of casting out will be through the bowels and the pores of the skin, unless obstructed by fears on the part of the patient or those interested.

When a patient passes quietly and non-resistingly from disease into health this intermediary stage will hardly be noticed, it being signified only by a slight mental disturbance, a sort of unreasonable irritation at things and people, accompanied by a few aches and "growing pains" in different parts of the body, especially those parts formerly diseased. These are but echoes of a past that is rapidly passing away from the patient's consciousness, and they are nothing in themselves, and the less the patient and healer notice them the better for the case.

The mental casting out will be marked by a confidential talk which may include secrets never divulged before. It may even be a sort of confessional, and the penitent may be filled with guilty remorse, and repentant tears flow freely. Let them flow, seeking only to check them by the true denial of the whole matter, silently given.

Confession to the healer is not necessary, and no healer should urge it, for to demand it is to assume the presence of evil, which assumption would decrease the effectiveness of your treatments.

Should there be an unconscious resistance to the Truth on the part of the patient there may appear to be fever and acute pains. This is because of fear, and to allay the fever and pain the healer speaks, coolly and calmly, true words of comfort : "There is nothing to fear. Peace ! be still," putting the soothing reassuring statements in silent utterances especially adapted to the mentality of the one needing help.

This is the treatment, the first one, given to all acute cases, such as pneumonia, and in accidents and sudden sharp pains. Wherever the condition is excitable and feverish speak slowly, softly, and soothingly, whether your word is silent or audible. Where the condition is fainting, dazed, or lethargic let your word be expressed vigorously, like a rousing command. In acute cases the fever or the pain should yield while the patient is in the presence of the healer, or, if it is an absent case, the healer should receive inward assurance that the case is reached.

Do not treat the case continuously, but let there be intervals of time the same length as the treatments. If there have been twenty minutes of silent treatment, then let there be twenty minutes of relaxation and trust, in which you turn your mind completely from the patient to restful, trustful subjects of attention. Then again give yourself to faithful prayer until the case begins to show response. When this is assured, then the case can be carried forward just as in chronic diseases.

Remember to be free from fear yourself. Meet every mental suggestion of evil with Truth, bearing in mind that every word spoken for yourself is helping the patient. You may be reflecting the fears of others, in which case they will come into mind, and a silent word to them will release you. Sometimes it will be well to have some one else treat you, especially if you are personally interested in your case.

In cases of children, deny the influence of the parents' or guardians' fears, and address these parties individually with the Truth that disperses fears, doubts, and unbeliefs.

Do not be moved by groans, or screams, or evil sights. Let no appearance of evil cause you to "lose your head" or grow faint-hearted, but under all circumstances keep your self-possession by remembering what is the Self and who has charge of the case. It is God who has called you to it, and God is taking care of His own.

Every one who turns to Truth for his healing, or through the love of another is brought under its influence, is the subject of a special Providence, and though all things were against him he can truly say, "The Lord is the strength of my life; of whom shall I be afraid?" Ps. 27:1.

A healer may have mental pictures while giving treatment. They should be looked upon as symbolical, and either disregarded or used as indicators of what statements will be most helpful to the case. Thus, if a coffin were seen, or some other symbol of death, it should mean that the healer speak fervent words for the manifestation of Life and Life more abundant. The sign means that error is dying not the patient, who is being called forth from the sepulchre of the old existence into the new Life and Health.

Painless childbirth is one of the blessings now manifest through the power and knowledge of Truth. To realize that the matrix is a most normal organ in its office and capable of great elasticity and muscular power is helpful in removing the false beliefs associated with the efforts of child-bearing.

Woman is under the law of Christ and no longer under the Adamic curse of multiplied conceptions and sorrowful travail. Babes represent spiritual ideas, and they can be brought forth without a struggle and in fullness of joy. The Christian world has been long in realizing this emancipation of woman expressed by Paul in I Timothy, second chapter, fifteenth verse : "She shall be saved in child-bearing, if they continue in faith and charity and holiness with sobriety."

The banishment of fear insures painless parturition by allowing all the organs to adjust themselves. Therefore let the same treatment be given in such cases as with any crisis, seeing all painful manifestations as only indicators that new ideas and expressions are seeking externalization, and need only our co-operation to cause the pain to vanish, and the true condition to be made a triumphant and happy visibility.

When giving the regular "week's treatment" proceed as upon the first day, substituting for the fifth step the following:

Make such denials and affirmations as are appropriate to the case. In the six-day course of treatment, the fourth day you deny that there is anything to fear, or any cause for guilt or remorse, or that there is any influence in the fears of others, and you affirm the protection of the Love of God and the presence of Almighty Trust in the power of Good, Life, Health, Peace, and Prosperity.

Sudden and painful attacks of "disease are among the easiest of the problems to be solved by mental healers. They almost invariably yield instantaneously, and are among the best proofs of the power of the Word to those who seek testimony through the senses.

A few such instances will be very helpful to the young healer in giving confidence in his or her word. And this very confidence will be a healing power in itself. When you have gained this, you will find that your very entrance into the sick room will allay pain. More than this, the moment their cases enter your mind they will begin to be better, and you will find that often for them simply to turn to you will relieve them.

Cases have been healed when the healer has received no message and given no special treatment. There has been a silent union and communion made even when the personalities of either healer or patient have not known it.

Lay up heavenly treasures of faith and love, and you will be an inexhaustible bank to draw upon for healing and help in every way.

LESSON XI. DIVINE UNDERSTANDING, OUR STRENGTH.

THE well-balanced mind manifests as evenness in temperament, wherein are no seasons of moodiness or moments of discouragement, down-heartedness, or gloom in any form. Students who have times when they feel melancholy have a "fit of the blues," hearts that are heavy when days are gray, bodies that feel themselves cumbersome and weary all these are the effects of believing oneself subject to ignorance and liable to foolishness. Such minds must be set free from self-depreciation, which rises from believing in superiority and inferiority. Contentment and self-sufficiency must be manifest through realizing the Lord to be our very Self.

Divine understanding gives strength and independence. He who turns to the secret place in his own nature for all knowledge will walk with God, and not be lame or halt in his mental going. "Stand upright on thy feet !" Learn to stand upon your own power of knowing Truth and interpreting life and Scripture, then your mental feet can walk, run, skip, dance, and go through every other performance, and yet keep their grace and self-mastery, for "the center of gravity will not fall without the base," the mind become unbalanced, or the feelings grow stolid and glum.

Discontent and the sense of uselessness are overcome by the power of Self-centering and ceasing to look outside for satisfaction and knowledge.

"Be strong and of a good courage," said Jehovah again and again to the children of Israel as they were preparing to enter into the promised land of Canaan (Deut. 31 :6, 7, 23 ; Josh. 1 :6, 9, 18). "Be strong and of a good courage, fear not nor be afraid of them : for the Lord thy God, he it is that doth go with thee; he will not fail thee, nor forsake thee."

Learn to associate understanding with strength, and. conversely, see that discouragement, weakness, and weariness are to be associated with ignorance and foolishness, and realize that the healing of depression and inefficiency lies in spiritual understanding.

Perfect freedom, that comes through knowing, manifests as divine, non-resistant independence of all earthly authority and all earthly forms, ceremonies, dogmas, and creeds. All knowledge must be looked for within oneself, and no matter who or what says a thing, when that authority is outside our own heart and mind we are only to accept it as the Spirit in us bears witness to it that it is true. Jesus says, "I receive not testimony from man" (John 5:34) ; and he also says, "Follow me." Luke: 959. So, since Jesus receives not the testimony of man, and we would follow him, neither are we to receive the testimony of man, but listen to the Father within, just as he did. "All thy children shall be taught of God." Is. 54:13. "Every man therefore that hath heard, and hath learned of the Father, cometh unto me," says Jesus (John 6:45).

The day, prophesied by Jeremiah, in which a man may say that he knows of himself that this is true, and does not believe it because of what any good man or any good book says, but because of the Christ in him, is now here. "After those days, saith the Lord, I will put my law in their inward parts and write it in their hearts; and will be their God, 'and they shall be my people. And they shall teach no more every man his neighbor, and every man his brother, saying, Know the Lord: for they shall all know me, from the least of them unto the greatest of them, saith the Lord." Jer. 31:33, 34.

Divine understanding gives one power to discern all teachings, and ability to divide the wheat from the chaff and keep only that which is true and spiritually profitable. You must trust to the "inspiration of the Almighty" (Job 32:8) in you in reading all books and in listening to all men. Trust in the omnipresent and omnipotent Truth makes us fearless and tolerant towards every claim to knowledge, and we cannot be deceived by sophistry nor misled by strange doctrines, for were we even to drink of most poisonous teaching we would receive only the innocent part of it, thus spiritually fulfilling the Christ-promise, "If they drink any deadly thing, it shall not hurt them." Mark 16:18.

The two greatest aids to an understanding of Scriptural texts are (1) the practice of applying Truth to all the common experiences of daily life and interpreting events from the standpoint of mental causation, and (2) listening to the Holy Spirit within you. Thus you can have every passage in the Scriptures explained, and you will see how all the apparently contradictory passages can be reconciled.

The Spirit of Truth is with you now, that Spirit that was promised by Jesus, and of which he said, "He dwelleth with you, and shall be in you" (John 14:17), and also "he will guide you into all truth" (John 16: 13) ; moreover "he shall teach you all things" (John 14: 26), and will "abide with you forever." John 14:16. This Spirit tells you the meaning of all Scripture, and whenever a text or story is interpreted truly through any other student, this Spirit will corroborate it, filling your heart with warm, harmonious assurances of its trueness.

How does the Spirit reconcile "God is angry with the wicked every day" (Ps. 7:11) with the Christ-thought, "he is kind unto the unthankful and to the evil" (Luke 6:35)? In this way: As long as people think they can act wickedly and contrary to the will of God, just so long will they believe that God is a God of wrath and punishment, or as John the Baptist preached, "He that believeth not the Son shall not see life ; but the wrath of God abideth on him." John 3:36. But Christ came to change men's beliefs about God and show them the loving Father instead of the angry God, and whoever believes the Christ-self, and follows His direction, will know God to be pure Love in which there is no anger ever.

The spirit of understanding shows us that all Scriptural passages which represent God as having passions like mortal men, and doing as men do, are an account of God's being and action as it appears to them men's ideas about God. When men repent, then God seems to repent, as in the case of Nineveh (Jonah 3:10). When men are tempted of their own lusts they, ascribing evil to God, say they are tempted of God (Jas. 1:13, 14). When men are hard and severe, rigid in discipline, and revengeful, their God is the same character to them. He that is loving and forgiving has a loving and forgiving father as his God.

God knows no evil and therefore does not permit evil. For God to recognize evil would be for God to think an evil thought, and to think with God is to give life and reality to the thought and to perpetuate it forever, for no thought of God's can ever be destroyed. God's mind is too pure to behold iniquity. "Thou art of purer eyes than to behold evil, and canst not look on iniquity." Hab. 1:13. God does not see the evil and imperfection in you, but only that which is the Good and the True in your being. Therefore it is with joy that we know, "Thou God seest me" and not with fear and shame.

It is because you are continually in the mind and heart of God that you are immortal. Your life is perpetually sustained by God loving you all the time. To recognize this is to be reconciled to God, spoken of so much in the Bible. To be reconciled to God is to see God and love Him, even as He sees and loves us. Since God does not recognize sin and evil it is not true to say that God permits these things to be. Such is the right view of God, and it stops all that useless questioning as to "why God lets so much sin and suffering be in the world." It is because God is not recognizing these things that their time is short and their apparent power temporal.

Can God ever be sorrowful or helpless in the presence of evil ? No. Yet one of these would be true if the good God were to behold evil and not annihilate it. "To the pure all things are pure." Titus 1:15. Who is so pure as God? God sees you as you really are pure, holy, true, sinless and this seeing is your salvation. God sees all things working together for His glory and honor, and His predestination and fore-ordination is that He has ordained that the Divine in each shall prove itself of His nature and being, and that the false and the untrue shall be proven pure nothingness, without place or power in the realm of appearances, even as in the realm of the Real. God knows all things that were, and are, and are to be, and He knows, and has always known, that the Real in us would triumph and be glorified, and that the false would finally take its place in "outer darkness," in nothingness.

The "elect" and the "chosen," spoken of in Scripture, is that One in each of us that came from God, and returns to God, and is in God now. It is the only One that enters into Heaven. "No man ascendeth up to heaven, but he that came down from heaven, even the Son of man, which is in heaven." John 3:13.

The "son of perdition" (John 17:12) is the false one of each of us, the personality, the man of flesh, the carnal. This one is cast away in Peter and in John just as much as in Judas. It was the son of perdition in Peter that Jesus spoke to when he said, "Get thee behind me, Satan: thou art an offence unto me: for thou savorest not the things that be of God, but those that be of men" (Matt. 16:23), and it was the Son of God in Peter to whom Jesus spoke words the very opposite in kind just previously: "Blessed art thou. Simon Barjona : for flesh and blood hath not revealed it unto thee, but my Father which is in heaven." Matt. 16:17.

Other names for "that man of sin" (2 Thes. 2:3) are "sons of Belial" (Judges 20:12, 13), which the children of Israel were called when in error; "children of the devil" (John 8:44); and "children of the wicked one" (Matt. 13:38), spoken of by Jesus in the parable of the wheat and the tares. God sows the divine Self, the children of the Kingdom, and apparently right beside this Real One is sown the false self, whose father is a lie (deception). These both grow together until the harvest, when the wheat (all the Truth in each) is gathered into His barns (the Kingdom of Heaven), and the false (the tares) in each of us is gathered together and burned in Love, the everlasting fires of God. This judgment is being passed continuously, and ever the True, the Good, is being separated from the false, the evil, and the Lord God in you is saying to the false, "Depart from me, I know you not whence ye are" (Luke 13:25, 27), and to the true. "Enter thou into the joy of thy Lord." Matt. 25:23. In the parable of the shepherd and his flock (Matt. 25:32), the sheep represent the pure, innocent, meek, gentle, peaceful thoughts ; the goats, the wild, unruly, aggressive, willful thoughts.

Into outer darkness (the nothing) and the bottomless pit (the nothing) are cast (Rev. 21:8) all fearful thoughts, all doubts (the unbelieving), all angry thoughts, all lies, and everything that "loveth and maketh a lie," Rev. 22:15.

Who is not glad to see this carried out in himself? "Purge me with hyssop, and I shall be clean: wash me, and I shall be whiter than snow." Ps. 51:7.

There is no superiority and inferiority in God we are all One, we are all equal, the first is as the last, and the greatest as the least. It is only when we look at ourselves as separate personalities that we see some one superior or inferior. All that was in Jesus is in you now, and all that is in you is in every magdalen that walks the land. The One that is equal in us all is the Christ, the only One.

Self-depreciation has no place in the true Self. Do not compare yourself with others, nor contrast the followers of Truth. Speak the truth each man to his neighbor and of his neighbor, which is : "There is only One in you that knows, and that One is the same in me and in all, and that One knows all things."

When the disciples went out upon their first ministry they had no dogma or creed to preach. Their first sending forth was by Jesus while he was yet with them, so they could not preach about a crucifixion upon Golgotha, nor the necessity of believing in such an event in order to be saved. Then what was their "preaching of the cross," as Paul expressed it in I Corinthians, first chapter, eighteenth verse? What was Paul's preaching of it? Was it an historical event he was talking about, or did he see that the crucifixion of Jesus was a symbol, just as he saw that the Jewish sacrifices of rams and bullocks were symbols?

The "preaching of the cross" with all the true disciples of Jesus was just the same as that of Jesus himself. And that preaching is found embodied in his words, "If any man will come after me, let him deny himself, and take up his cross, and follow me." Matt. 16:24. The preaching of the cross is the teaching of the denial of the personality, the material universe, and the principle of evil, or, in ecclesiastical language, it is the denial of "the world, the flesh, and the devil." That which is the means by which you deny is called the Cross. To "cross out" is to cancel, and as long as there seems to be anything to be cancelled we must have our cross with us, which Paul calls "the power of God."

When you successfully deny yourself by right mental practice and a selfless life, you reach that place where you can lay down your body at will, and you can take it up again. "I have power to lay it down, and I have power to take it again." John 10:18. Then "take up your cross" in this case your personality (the body is often called the cross), that by which you arc visible to mortals, and by which you can deny in the hearing and sight of men "and follow me." That is, "Behold, I cast out devils, and I do cures to-day and to-morrow, and the third day I shall be perfected. Nevertheless I must walk to-day and to-morrow, and the day following." Luke 13: 32, 33. To follow Christ we must "walk" until we realize the word of the Father, "I have finished the work which thou gavest me to do." John 17:4. This is to know, in the flesh, our perfection, the glory which we had with the Father before the world was. To take up the cross daily is to deny something of the world, the personality, and evil every day. It is well not to have any preference between denial and affirmation, but to see that these each and both be used. Cross and crown they are. If one does not deny the false self, its world, and its evil, then one cannot effectually affirm the true Self, its kingdom, and its righteousness. The wise have said, "No cross, no

Dominion over disease and decay and freedom from sinning ultimate in victory over death. Dying is no part of life, and, according to the Genesis account, was not in the experience of men until they were disobedient to the divine instruction: "The tree of the knowledge of good and evil, thou shalt not eat of it : for in the day that thou eatest thereof thou shalt surely die." Gen. 2:17.

The greatest work of Jesus' ministry was the triumph over death, his other works, such as healing diseases and emancipating from sin, being subservient to that end and necessary first-steps in the great demonstration.

When asked to give a sign peculiar to his teaching (Matt. 12:38-41) Jesus gave Jonah's deliverance from hell and death as an example of the one sign that should be given by him to mankind. He allowed himself to be murdered, dying the most disgraceful death a criminal can suffer. "No man taketh it [my life] from me, but I lay it down of myself. I have power to lay it down, and I have power to take it again. This commandment have I received of my Father." John 10:18. This he did that there might be a recorded proof of man's dominion over death. So that even if a spiritually instructed man from any cause become hypnotized into death, he there may remember himself, and break the mesmeric spell, and resuscitate himself by the power of God in him.

Through unfaith the professors of Christianity during these many centuries have lost or obscured this masterly teaching of the Lord Christ by attributing his promises of life eternal to a future world. If one reads his words upon this divine gift and power of everlasting life (John 6:31-63) with the true light upon them, he will see that Jesus did not mean "spiritual death" at all. He says, "Your fathers did eat manna in the wilderness, and are dead" Did he mean that Moses, Joshua, Caleb, Aaron, and many other righteous Israelites were spiritually dead? No. He referred to their physical death. "I am the living bread which came down from heaven : if any man eat of this bread, he shall live forever." John 6:51. He said to Martha: "I am the resurrection, and the life : he that believeth in me, though he were dead, yet shall he live : and whosoever liveth and believeth in me shall never die. Believest thou this?" John 11:25, 26. Yet Martha, type of Christian stolidity, did not understand. Instead of grasping his great teaching about victory over death, she but reiterated her convictions of his Christhood.

"Putting on incorruption" is the term with which Paul describes the divine alchemy that takes place in the human body which is going through the regeneration and transmutation of each cell from a center of change and decay to one of purity and life . All the tissues, fluids, and elements of the physical body are subject to every thought of mind. As the mind realizes the unsubstantiality of matter and the readiness of flesh to obey thought, ideas will be held that will beautify even the earthly form, causing it to express grace, youthfulness, strength, purity, according to the individual desire of the one it represents. It can be retained in the sight of men and function in the midst of humanity as long as its possessor wishes, and, when its master wills, disappear as the mirage withdraws with the setting of the sun.

Figuratively speaking, you are the sun, and the physical body is but one of the many pictures your imagining power is forming, revealing, and causing to disappear.

It is the "man of sin" of whom it is said that his "years are three-score years and ten." Ps. 90:10. As we journey back to our Eden ("and truly, if they had been mindful of that country from whence they came out, they might have had opportunity to have returned" Heb. 11:15) we shall return to the great age of the patriarchs, as it is promised, "For as the days of a tree are the days of my people, and mine elect shall long enjoy the work of their hands." Is. 65:22.

The apostle Paul taught the transmutation of the body, and that we rise from the dead while still in the garment of flesh (1 Cor. 15:47-58). "We shall not all sleep, but we shall all be changed." 1 Cor. 15:51. "For we that are in this tabernacle do groan, being burdened: not for that we would be unclothed, but clothed upon, that mortality might be swallowed up of life." 2 Cor. 5:4. "Therefore if any man be in Christ, he is a new creature: old things are passed away; behold, all things are become new" 2 Cor. 5:17. "Ourselves also, which have the first fruits of the Spirit, even we ourselves groan within ourselves, waiting for the adoption, to wit the redemption of our body." Rom. 8:23. "And I pray God your whole spirit and soul and body be preserved blameless unto the coming of our Lord Jesus Christ" 1 Thes. 5:23.

Those who have "passed away" from the physical plane, the so-called dead, are not barred from the teachings of Truth thereby. They have simply retired into the mental regions of the world. Yet they are not in advance of the rest of humanity because of their experience. If they will but receive the Truth as it is given in their own realm of thinking they, too, can identify themselves with the Highest, overcome mortality's errors and await in peaceful trust the consummation of the healing of the whole world, when the veil that separates the psychic realm from the physical shall be rent in twain, and the two become as one. This is the age to come, called the Second Coming of Christ, when each shall be God's Christ, even as Jesus was and is.

The forms and ceremonies of the church are all symbolical of interior processes. As external forms they are nothing at all, and have no power in themselves. Taken alone they are "the letter that killeth." The reality is in the heart and mind. Ceremonies without accompanying heart correspondences are like words without thought, and of them the assassin-king in Hamlet says when trying to pray:

My words fly up, my thoughts remain below :
Words without thoughts, never to heaven go.

The real baptism is within, and no rite of baptism is effectual that is not one with the same process performed in the heart (Lesson 2). No one need to be externally baptized unless he be led of the Holy Spirit so to do. Nevertheless if one wishes to be baptized, let no one stand in that one's way. So also with every other ordinance and form of the church.

The true communion of the Lord's Supper is eating the words of Truth and drinking the words of Life.

To eat and drink of the flesh and blood of Jesus Christ is to let his spirit fill you, and to lead his Life by keeping his sayings in thought, word, and deed.

In the great lesson which he gave upon the communion (John 6:47-63) Jesus plainly reveals his mystic statement, "Except ye eat the flesh of the Son of man and drink his blood ye have no life in you," by the closing words of his discourse, "It is the spirit that quickeneth ; the flesh profiteth nothing : the words that I speak unto you, they are spirit and they are life."

He who eats and drinks the words of Christ partakes of the communion daily. Every time he eats and drinks outwardly he can sup with the Lord by realizing that he does not eat material food, but in spirit and in truth is receiving and incorporating into his very being the substance of God.

Every act of the life can be holy. "Whatsoever ye do, do it from the soul, as unto the Lord, and not unto men." Col. 3:23. He that realizes the cleansing of the word of Truth is baptized every time he washes his hands or enters his bath. The true "grace" to breathe before each meal is the consciousness that in reality one is identifying himself with the substance (spirit) and creative power (life) of God.

The fasting of the saints arose from their continual denial of the world, the flesh, and the devil. When filled with the bread and wine of the Spirit the devotee often finds himself having no appetite for material food, and so does not eat, nor care to eat. Then the world sees him fasting. He is not fasting to become spiritual, but because he has become spiritual he is fasting.

"Is not this the fast that I have chosen? to loose the bands of wickedness, to undo the heavy burdens, and to let the oppressed go free, and that ye break every yoke ? ... Is it not to deal thy bread to the hungry, and that thou bring the poor that are cast out to thy house? when thou seest the naked, that thou cover him; and that thou hide not thyself from thine own flesh?" Is. 58:6, 7.

It is divine understanding that enables us to see all things in their true light, and to rely upon ourselves for all teaching and interpretation. As we look within for all our instruction, we shall see that all the world is contributing to us of its wealth of knowledge without our seeking it or asking for it, for outward teachers, whether they are persons or books, are symbols of certain thoughts held in the mind. Say to yourself, "God reveals that to me," and soon some person comes along and speaks the very word you are to hear it may be a sentence, or a course of lectures. Say to yourself, "God reveals that to me," and you pick up just the book you should, or read the very article in magazine or newspaper you should. It is wisdom not to ascribe any of your learning to an earthly teacher or an earthly book, but continue in the thought forever, "I am taught of God only."

There are no burdens in the spiritual consciousness. "Cast thy burden on the Lord*' (Ps. 55 122) and know that by so doing you make nothing of it, for God is not burdened with heavy cares and weary work. To cast your burden upon the Lord is as though it were dropped into the bottomless pit. When you have thus thrown off this sense of weighty responsibility see that you do not take it again.

"Bear ye one another's burdens" by making nothing of them.

If, at times, you find yourself in the "slough of despond" and cannot account for your state of mind, you may be reflecting some one's despondency, and you can come quickly out by sending the word of courage, strength, and knowledge to some one who appears to be under the cloud of sorrow or misfortune. If you know no such one, then radiate quickening, invigorating beams of wisdom to the whole world, and some drooping heart will receive refreshment, and return an answering chord of relief that will set you free.

If you ever feel discouraged over a case, treat your patient for secret discouragement, or yourself for the belief of the lack of knowledge and of power.

In the regular order of six-day course of treatment this is the fifth stage of unfoldment, generally an appearance of weakness, weariness, and discouragement, and therefore the especial word is that which brings realization of the inner source of strength and knowledge, the inexhaustible supply of life, health, and goodness, the freedom from every burden.

"Be not weary in well doing." 2 Thes. 3:13.

LESSON XII. DIVINE COMPLETENESS, OUR SATISFACTION.

ALL language descriptive of God and the Soul is, at best, but figurative. So the enlightened man does not cavil at the use of limited terms to express spiritual processes. He knows that,

The tau [the word] that can be tau-ed [worded] is not the Eternal Tau [The Word]. Lao-Tse.

The name that can be named is not the Eternal Name. And he can speak of the changeless verities of God as he wills, and not be deceived by the words he uses. Thus, much is said by inspired teachers of the awakening of the Soul, yet the Soul never sleeps. The Psalmist cries, "Awake, why sleepest thou, O Lord?" (Ps. 44:23), and yet he truly knows, "He that keepeth Israel shall neither slumber nor sleep." Ps. 12:14. The true Self is ever awake and conscious of itself and the Truth. This knowledge is eternal peace and bliss, and to abide in it is rest and satisfaction always, as it is written, "I shall be satisfied when I awake with thy likeness." Ps. 17:15.

To awaken is to come to the consciousness of who we are and where we are. We are now awake to the knowledge that we are holy, spiritual Being, and that we are surrounded by the Kingdom of Heaven, that we have ever been what we are now, and God's perfect world is the only true realm, and in it is nothing of wrong or of injury and pain. It is restful joy to maintain this true cognition of our Self, and dissatisfaction is impossible to him who remembers his divinity and its omnipotence.

The Soul knows that it is free from the delusions of sense, that illusion has never deceived it, and therefore it has neither been attracted nor repelled by the changeable, unreal forms of mortality. The Soul does not need experiences in matter in order to receive knowledge. She knows all things now. Nothing is true of your Soul that is not true of God. God is not evolved, neither are you. God, the Perfect, does not progress from a state of ignorance and not-being to one of knowledge and being, neither do you. Progression is an appearance, the representation of that eternal joyous going from glory to glory, the "many mansions" of our "Father's house," those manifestations whose number is infinity and whose beauties are transcendently varied and yet all One, that is, God.

As the panorama of existence passes before the gaze of the emancipated devotee he sees :

"I am all that I have ever loved in this : I am the beautiful, the noble, the pure, the grand that is mirrored about me. In the great harmonies, I sing; in the weavings of the sunlight through hue and form, I glide in every heart that loves; I am the lover ; in every dear one, I am the beloved. I laugh in the innocent child, I think in the masterful reasoner. All men love me and there is none unloved of me. Life is a great symphony, and I am the musician ; an enchanting romance, and I am the romancer.

"I am in my story or not, as I will never entangled, yet lavishing my whole being upon my holy creation ; doing nothing by halves, for my Love gives its whole life, service, and being to its Beloved. In peace and in joy, henceforth, shall I lead my own to the heights of bliss. By comforting words, by easy paths, shall I invite and guide each and every heart which seeks that which I am into the happiness which is mine, 'eternal in the heavens.' "

Then is it revealed to the devotee how he, too, has been led all the way along to his deliverance. He learns that all nature is in a friendly conspiracy to assist him and to contribute to his happiness, and to the ultimate emancipation of all.

Nothing happens by chance in man's life. Great laws are back of every movement he makes. What you did that time when you took the step that has seemed such a mistake was the outcome of the myriads of thoughts that went before. The tendencies of character obey that natural law, so familiar in mechanics, of moving along the line of the least resistance. With the desires you had, and the knowledge you possessed, you could not have done otherwise than you did. Nevertheless, even of our mistakes the Good can and does make advantages to us. Watch for the Good in all the events of your life. Be alert to discover what new realization the Spirit is presenting to you, that your joy may be increased. Every personality that walks beside you in life's journey is as a jewel casket holding an entrancing treasure which now and then is opened for whomsoever will to see. Whoever sees the priceless interior of any nature, be its external even passingly foolish or uncouth, will never forget, but will love that one, and having truly loved once, will love "unto the end." John 13:1.

The Christ in giving life to the world gives Love. It wells up in the heart spontaneously, and as your cup runs over with its bounty your eyes are opened to see the ideal in some one, and you exalt that one to the very throne of deity. Your ecstasy is holy, and in your wisdom you see that this loved one is a means of holding the great overflow of divine joy, as glasses hold the effervescing wine, until such time as the great love can be lifted up into the Universal Presence wherein all are loved with the same fervor and bliss. The highest office of the earthly institution of marriage is to afford an orderly, serene, happy way up which the human love may mount to that all-absorbing divine Love of God, that unspeakable happiness about whose charms poet an prophet have never ceased to sing since first Love said, "Let there be light."

The Hindu scriptures say :

Verily a husband is not dear that you may love the husband, but that you may love the self, for that is a husband dear. Verily a wife is not dear that you may love the wife, but that you may love the self, for that is the wife dear. Verily the worlds are not dear that you may love the worlds, but that you may love the self, for that are the worlds dear. Verily creatures are not dear that you may love the creatures, but that you may love the self, for that are creatures dear.

He who would increase in spirituality and in powers to do the works of Christ, let him increase in love, for greater than knowing is love, greater than faith is love. There is nothing that love cannot do. Your whole being is filled with love now you are a concentration of desire, which is but a form of love. Desire brought you into manifestation, and holds you there, and governs all your steps just give avenues and vehicle to the great love which you have. "Love is of God; and every one that loveth is born of God, and knoweth God." 1 John 4:7.

The Soul is complete. It is not dual, it is One. It has never been divided into sexes, and therefore it is not seeking a mate. The appearance of sex is a delusion, part of the masquerading in which the Self is denied and the claim of being separated from our Beloved is setup. The petty differences that lie in the mind associated with belief in duality fall away, and we rise above the weaknesses of sexuality as we see our Soul. The wild, eager search of men and women for companions who shall understand them and appreciate their true nature is really the search after God. And satisfaction comes only as God is found, and the Holy One seen to be our real bride, our real husband. "For thy Maker is thine husband; the Lord of Hosts is his name ; and thy Redeemer the Holy One of Israel ; The God of the whole earth shall he be called" Is. 54:5.

The earthly marriage can represent the heavenly union, and if those who find themselves in this relation but exalt its every department to the highest and holiest place, they can make of it a perpetual sacrament and a means of developing the hidden beauties of their nature through abiding in chastity, gentleness, love-service, patience, and reverence towards the Lord in each.

Those who give all their desires and powers to God no longer generate after the flesh but after the Spirit, which is the re-generation. Birth, marriage, and death are but different forms of the same proceeding. Each has a mystical significance describing a spiritual reality. You are Spirit, therefore, in reality, you were never born, neither do you marry, neither shall you die any more, even as the Lord Christ has said: "They which shall be accounted worthy to obtain that world, and the resurrection from the dead, neither marry nor are given in marriage: neither can they die any more; for they are equal unto the angels; and are the children of God." Luke 20:35, 36.

Wise men, inspired of the One, have taught that the Lord of all is the Unnameable, and that no one name can comprehend all that It is, and that no one statement of Truth can convey the knowledge and beauty of the Divine Presence. The mind that is the most efficient vehicle in bringing one to the apprehension of Deity must be supremely elastic and supple in its dealings with the many contradictory statements made concerning "Him that is without a second."

The mind swings between such extreme utterances as "God is All" and "God is the Nothing," and finds the unity of the extremes, and rests in conscious poise and ecstasy of realization. It sees that there is only God, and the Nothing is the receptivity of the divine nature, the Motherhood of God, and the All is the Fatherhood of God. The All is ever filling the Nothing, and this full-filling is manifestation and creation. Nature is the holy Mother, pure nothingness, the void, without whom there could be no bringing forth. She is God, the immaculate Virgin that all womanhood typifies. Her emptiness ever draws the divine substance into manifestation. She is never known as the Nothing, but by the name of her Lord. All creation reveals her mystery ; the sap rushes up the trees because her vacuum precedes it, the breath flows into the lungs because of the emptiness, there is no movement of currents of air or water, of rock or fire, but must have a vacancy to cause its motion.

Of this sweet Mother of us all the mystic sings :

There was something chaotic in nature which existed before heaven and earth. It was still. It was void. It stood alone, and was not changed. It pervaded everywhere, and was not endangered. It may be regarded as the Mother of the Universe. I know not its name; but I give it the title of "Tau." Lao-Tse.

The heavenly Nothing is manifest in us as humility and meekness and lowliness of heart. This is the philosophy of taking the lowest place, and thereby being exalted; of truly retiring, and in consequence being made prominent ; of the honor conferred upon the modest ; of the lowly being raised up. When the feminine (the negative) of your nature is discovered, the masculine (the positive) cannot be suppressed; creation is inevitable.

He who knows the masculine and keeps the feminine, will be the whole world's channel, (*. e., the center of universal attraction.) Tao-teh-king, with translator's commentary.

All Good rushes to you, all manifestation seeks to express its joy, its

All The Way

Foreword

THOSE who have made up their minds to go on to the Ascension, taking all the steps essential to that attainment, should read each chapter and verse carefully and prayerfully. For there is a teaching for each Candidate which is beneath the words and unwritten and, to catch that instruction, there must be a conscious openness to the TEACHER WITHIN.

The writing of this Handbook on ALL THE Way has not been by subject or by any fixed order that human intellect might dictate, but on the contrary. For each chapter was written as the substance came to me with apparent repetitions, and some disconnected and irrelevant presentations, because of leaving the construction wholly to the Spirit that guides the Candidate into all the truth that belongs to achieving the Christ goal.

The paragraphs are numbered as well as the chapters for convenience in referring to specific instruction,

God grant that many will be led to commune with themselves and, by the power of their own great Self, determine to reach the Heights. Any communication from you, dear Reader, as to your experiences and aspirations as well as obstacles in the Path upon which your feet shall henceforth walk, will be welcome and held in sacred confidence.

Let us ever remember that none could make this attainment in his own strength. It is God that walks the Way in us and is our Almighty Power to attain the Heights. To him only belongs the glory.

I

And there went great multitudes with him: and he turned, and said unto them.

If any man come to me and hate not his father, and mother, and wife, and children, and brethren, and sisters, yea, and his own life also, he cannot be my disciple.

And whosoever doth not bear his cross, and come after me, cannot be my disciple.

For which of you, intending to build a tower, sitteth not down first, and counteth the cost, whether he have sufficient to finish it?

Lest haply, after he hath laid the foundation, and is not able to finish it, all that behold it begin to mock him.

Saying, This man began to build, and was not able to finish.

Or what king, going to make war against another king, sitteth not down first, and consulteth whether he be able with ten thousand to meet him that cometh against him with twenty thousand.

Or else, while the other is yet a great way off, he sendeth an embassage, and desireth conditions of peace.

So likewise, whosoever he be of you that forsaketh not all that he hath, he cannot be my disciple. — Luke 14:25-33.

EVERYONE who is contemplating going forward in the Christ Life to its glorious ultimate must begin to consider all that it means. It means all for All.

2 Therefore Jesus presents it very strongly, that unless you can, in seeking to do the will and work of Christ, be indifferent to relatives, even to the one who has been dearest, and indifferent to your own life, you cannot follow the Master to the heights.

3 Holding to one's possessions, to one's pleasures, to one's duty to relatives, has kept many an earnest heart from making the attainment — the price,

"all that he hath," has been kept back.

4 He who sets out upon the Way of the Christ begins to lay the foundation of a Tower, which is the new body, the incorruptible body in which he can achieve the Ascension. To build upon that foundation a finished structure, he must have every stone of the Christ doctrine, alert to reject none lest he miss "the head of the corner," and therefore find himself among the many who shall strive to enter in and shall not be able,

5 This Walk with God means a consciousness in the outer (the body) and a consciousness within (the character). The king, your aspiring self, must consider whether it has the equipment to fight the carnal self that seems so strong. And if there seems something lacking one must either fight like David about to meet Goliath, casting oneself wholly upon God, or must take the whole message of the Christ of non-resistance and "agreeing with thine adversary," not warring at all but winning over evil with good.

6 The Christ Way is bearing your cross instead of rebelling and fighting it. The carnal self seems to cross the self that is aspiring to be one with the true Self. The old, violent way was to fight it, beating and otherwise punishing it unmercifully — the crucifixion that ended in death of the body. But Jesus was crucified literally once for all people, and we who follow him to the Ascension now "take up (elevate) our cross and follow" him.

7 So also other things that humiliate, persecute and torment one are crosses, not to be fought nor run away from, but to be lifted as Moses lifted the brazen serpent in the wilderness under the Lord's direction, and it healed all those who had been bitten by serpents, when they obediently "looked up" to it.

8 Every relative, friend or other personality must be secondary to the Life. The measure of one's freedom from relatives and other people is indicated by the amount of disturbance that is made within us by the contemplation of their disapproval or misunderstanding of us, or their loss through defection, treachery or death. Can we still realize the immortal Life of them and

ourselves? Do we continue to hold our peace and trust the Best in them? Let go I Give up! Loosen every chain.

9 "Who is my mother, or my brethren? Whosoever shall do the will of God, the same is my brother, my sister, and my mother," (Mark 3:33-35). "And call no man your father upon the earth: for one is your Father, which is in heaven," (Matt. 23:9).

10 "If any man come to me and hate not his . . ." (Luke 14:26); the word "hate" is not a good translation of the Greek word which means "to love less." For these relatives are our "neighbors" whom we are enjoined to love as ourselves, the Second Commandment, which "is like unto the First."

The significance is this, that when it comes to a choice, and we take our love for, or duty to, our relatives instead of the Way which is plainly to follow some direction of the Christ, then we cannot follow him all the Way.

11 Duty, even what seems a most sacred duty, must not interfere. Nothing was more binding in the heart of a filial Hebrew than to observe the last sacred rites in the burial of a parent. Yet the Master commanded one of his followers to

"Let the dead bury their dead, but go thou and preach the kingdom of God," (Luke 9:59, 60).

12 Not even sentiment shall enter in, not old observances of the ceremonies and habits that connect one with the former relationships shall interfere with the direct call to go forward in this upward Way.

13 Another follower of Jesus wished to turn back, to ceremoniously bid his people farewell, thus making himself liable to their influence and placing a stumbling block in his way. To him Jesus replies:

"No man, having put his hand to the plough, and looking back, is fit for the kingdom of God," (Luke 9:62).

14 "Go thou and preach the kingdom of God," is the word to all who are learning there is but one business in life, our heavenly Father's business. "Wist ye not that I must be about my Father's business?" (Luke 2:49).

15 "Labour not for the meat that perisheth, but for that meat which endureth unto everlasting life" (John 6:27), and he called his disciples from their fish nets and they dropped them where they were and followed him. He said to Matthew, the publican, as he sat at the money-changer's table, "Follow me," and he rose then and there and left his table as it was, and followed him.

16 No earthly business must stand in the way when the Master calls, even though that business be one's very life. No cares of the household should keep one from sitting at the Master's feet and serving him in the way he would be served, in ministering Truth to a hungry world.

17 We remember Jesus' rebuke of the fretful and complaining Martha, burdened with much serving, when she would take Mary away from listening to the message of Truth:

"Martha, Martha, thou art careful and troubled about many things: but one thing is needful: and Mary hath chosen that good part, which shall not be taken away from her," (Luke 10:38-42).

18 There is but one work for those who are walking the earthly road for the last time, and the sooner and the fuller such enter into this work of teaching the nations the Christ life, the more quickly they will advance in the heavenly Way and finish all earth's sorrows and hardships.

19 Meditation upon Jesus' words as our very own establishes the state of mind that will outpicture in the most direct and easiest way, the means and method of external accomplishment:

"To this end was I born, and for this cause came I into the world, that I should bear witness unto the truth. Every one that is of the truth heareth my voice," (John 18:37).

"I must work the works of him that sent me, while it is day: the night cometh when no man can work," (John 9:4).

"Say not ye, There are yet four months, and then cometh harvest. Behold, I say unto you, Lift up your eyes and look on the fields; for they are white already to harvest."

"The harvest truly is great, but the labourers are few: pray ye therefore the Lord of the harvest, that he would send forth labourers into his harvest," {John 4:35 and Luke 10:2).

"My Father worketh hitherto and I work," (John 5:17).

"Take no thought how or what ye shall speak: for it shall be given you in that same hour what ye shall speak. For it is not ye that speak, but the Spirit of your Father which speaketh in you," (Matt. 10:19, 20).

"The words that I speak unto you, I speak not of myself: but the Father that dwelleth in me, he doeth the works," (John 14:10).

"My meat is to do the will of him that sent me and to finish his work," (John 4:34).

"It is finished," (John 19:30).

20 And the work which Christ has given you to do? Six directions were given to the original twelve with the injunction that they were to teach others to do all that he had told them to do: "Go ye therefore and teach all nations . . . teaching them to observe all things whatsoever I have commanded you," (Matt. 28:19, 20).

The six directions are (Matt. 10:7, 8) :

1 Go, preach, saying, The kingdom of heaven is at hand.

2 Heal the sick.

3 Cleanse the lepers.

4 Raise the dead.

5 Cast out devils.

6 Freely ye have received, freely give.

21 The direction "Freely give" is especially stressed by the Master. For each one that enters the Way must learn early that God alone is our support and the means of our supply, and that all that we do should be without a thought of compensation from those benefited.

22 This going forth into the highways and byways of the world without thought of whereby we shall be fed, clothed or housed is a splendid adventure more fraught with surprises and marvellous achievements than those of the knights of old, whether Crusaders or mere adventurers.

23 We need no backing but the Holy Spirit, none to call us and ordain us but the Voice of Jesus Christ within us. And God will make our word and our work, good.

24 In all ways we loosen our minds from dependence upon worldly methods for our support and from looking to personalities to supply us or uphold us. We free ourselves from looking to our own work, whether spiritual or material, as our means of supply.

25 All attachment to money ceases with those who walk the Way; every one holding himself ready, no matter how great or how small or how precious his possessions may be, to "sell that ye have and give alms." Such a state of mind provides a perpetual wealth, "bags that wax not old, a treasure in the heavens that faileth not," (Luke 12:33).

26 We cannot be divided in our thoughts, feelings and works between worldly things and methods and those of the Spirit, one or the other will

suffer neglect and we shall make a success of neither. "No man can serve two masters: for either he will hate the one and love the other; or else he will hold to the one and despise the other. Ye cannot serve God and mammon. Therefore I say unto you, Take no thought for your life, what ye shall eat or what ye shall drink; nor yet for your body what ye shall put on," (Matt. 6:24, 25).

27 Of the two masters God is the one and money is the other. To try to serve both results in being indifferent to God ("hating the One") and worshipping money or giving it power and respect ("loving the other") or on the other hand, to try to serve both God and money, will be to attempt to live the spiritual life ("hold to the One") and to have such a contempt for money ("despise the other") as to be impractical in demonstrating prosperity.

28 The only way is to give all power, all thought, all respect and all place to God and let money follow that true consciousness as its natural shadow. So shall you be "seeking first the kingdom of God and his righteousness" and seeing "all these things" after which the worldly people seek "added unto you," (Matt. 6:33).

II

Behold I shew you a mystery; We shall not all sleep, but we shall all be changed.

In a moment, in the twinkling of an eye, at the last trump: far the trumpet shall sound, and the dead shall be raised incorruptible, and we shall be changed.

For this corruptible must put on incorruption, and this mortal must put on immortality.

So when this corruptible shall have put on incorruption, and this mortal shall have put on immortality, then shall be brought to pass the saying that is written, Death is swallowed up in victory.

O death, where is thy sting? O grave, where is thy victory?

The sting of death is sin; and the strength of sin is the law.

But thanks be to God, which giveth us the victory through our Lord Jesus Christ.

Therefore, my beloved brethren, be ye steadfast, unmoveable, always abounding in the work of the Lord, for as much as ye know that your labour is not vain in the Lord.— 1 Cor. 15:51-58.

1 The Way of the Christ is called in Isaiah 35:8, "The way of holiness." The prophet declares that "the unclean shall not pass over it but it shall be for those," that is, whoever enters that path of regeneration begins to be clean with his first step and, in order to progress ("pass over it") he must grow cleaner with every step.

2 Health is one of the requisites of the Candidate: every cell that has been liable to corruption must be cleansed of all such tendency and become, in form and substance, absolutely without corruption.

3 Therefore an education of complete purity begins in the feeling and thinking nature. Every lustful thought is arrested instantly. "You are none of mine," said one faithful student who began to see that the unwelcome suggestions coming to him did not originate with him. And the thoughts receded like the voice of a dream.

4 Every involuntary response in the body to a lustful suggestion is arrested, while communion begins silently with the Holy One within, our incorruptible Self.

5 Such an inner work begins the cleansing of the cells of the body. Whatever appearance of corruption may then force itself upon one's notice must be treated as though it were the whole body, rising from the dead.

6 A faithful demonstration with a single cell, is the uplifting (raising up or resurrection) of all the cells — the whole body. Therefore walk honestly, in

purity and in strength, from one incorruptible expression to another, until this whole body is "clothed upon with our house which is from heaven," (2 Cor. 5:2).

7 Perpetual youth is another requisite of those who are Candidates for the Christ attainment. "His flesh shall be fresher than a child's: he shall return to the days of his youth," (Job 33:25).

8 It matters not how many years may seem to have accumulated, let the Candidate but become young in heart and mind through remembering that the True Self is ever youthful (even while it is the Ancient of Days) and thereupon the body will begin to show renewal, and the whole being be filled with interest, enthusiasm, joy and strength.

9 It is promised that those who serve their God-Self shall renew their strength (Is. 40:31) ; they shall know no weariness; they shall cast their burdens upon the Lord; they shall not fail nor faint nor lose courage, but they "shall renew their youth like the eagle's" (the phoenix) ; and all these things are looked for in this Path of wisdom.

10 For the Way of the Christ is a joyous road wherein all the world's pleasures return to their innocence, purity and full zest. "They shall obtain joy and gladness, and sorrow and sighing shall flee away," (Is. 35:10). For Christ's way is truly the path of Wisdom, of whom it is written, "Her ways are ways of pleasantness and all her paths are peace," (Prov. 3:17).

1 Take every tear as a sign that some of the old life remains, and begin to purge the memory of its gloomy pictures and imaginations; heal the feelings of false sensitiveness, self-pity and the sense of the reality of the wrongs and griefs of mortality. Tenderness and sweet sympathy and compassion are Christ powers that act most perfectly when free from the weakness of tears.

12 The Way of Christ is all joy and all that walk it should walk in peace and happiness, adhering as faithfully to these expressions of the true Life, as the ancient religionists held to morality and goodness.

13 "In the way of righteousness is life; and in the pathway thereof there is no death" (Prov. 12:28) and all meditation upon death is finished. There is no looking forward to it as a release, nor is there any fear of death and what will follow.

14 "I AM the Door" and "I Am the Life," says the Christ, therefore Life is the Door and not death. Every Candidate should press on ardently to the Door of the Christ Life to pass quickly to the powers of the Ascension. For none can serve God and humanity ; so effectually and efficiently as those who are free to function with their whole being upon any, and all, planes, a power in which Jesus Christ dwells now who, describing that state, declared "All power is given unto me in heaven and in earth," (Matt. 28:18).

'15 "But some doubt," questioning their ability to reach the goal. Let them then seek to live the long life, even the patriarchal age, and use each year with all faithfulness to surmount unbelief and let God work out his own divine desire concerning them.

16 More than anything else, seek to be infused with the divine breath called the Holy Spirit. This is the baptism that brings about all things. It is the instantaneous and universal working of the whole of Heaven in Man.

17 Prayer is the one supreme instrument given to man by God for all attainment. "Pray without ceasing." "Watch and pray always." "This Spirit itself maketh intercession for us."

18 Prayer is the Word of God. It is God speaking to God. It is the Breath of God that is back of our physical breath, and when we are alert in consciousness of prayer or breathing from God, if our physical breath were suspended, we would continue life in this physical form through the Soul-breath until the physical breath should again be free.

19 "Tarry ye in the city of Jerusalem" — abide in spiritual and moral form and trueness, "until ye be endued with power from on high," (Luke 24:52). "Then returned they unto Jerusalem" and "all continued with one accord in prayer and supplication" (Acts 1 :12, 14) "and when the day of Pentecost

was fully come, they were all with one accord in one place, and suddenly there came a sound from heaven as of a rushing mighty wind, and it filled all the house where they were sitting. And there appeared unto them cloven tongues like as of fire and it sat upon each of them. And they were all filled with the Holy Ghost," (Acts 2:1 to 4).

"If ye then being evil know how to give good gifts to your children: how much more shall your heavenly Father give the Holy Spirit to them that ask him."

20 Forty days had the disciples communed with the resurrected Jesus Christ, upon the "things pertaining to the kingdom of God," (Acts 1 :3), and then they witnessed his "taking up." And, following his command, they stayed close in Jerusalem abiding and praying with one accord for ten days, and on the Fiftieth Day after the Passover week (from the day of the Resurrection) the same baptism descended upon the disciples that came upon Jesus as he went up out of the water-baptism of John the Baptist, (Mark 1:10, 11).

Meditate upon this initiation of those who walk all the way with Christ, and pray and commune with the Spirit and wait on the Lord until you know yourself "endued with power from on high."

III

They which shall be accounted worthy to obtain that world, and the resurrection from the dead, neither marry, nor are given in marriage. — Luke 20:35.

Behold the bridegroom cometh; go ye out to meet him. —Matt. 25 :6.

Let your loins be girded about, and your lights burning; and ye yourselves like unto men that wait for their Lord, when he will return from the wedding; that when he cometh and knocketh, they may open unto him immediately.— Luke 12:35, 36.

And the Spirit and the bride say. Come. And let him that heareth say, Come. — Rev. 22:17.

All men cannot receive this saying, save they to whom it is given. For there are some eunuchs, which were so born from their mother's womb: and there are some eunuchs, which were made eunuchs of men: and there be eunuchs, which have made themselves eunuchs for the kingdom of heaven's sake. He that is able to receive it, let him receive it. — Matt. 19:11, 12.

Strive to enter in at the strait gate; for many, I say unto you, will seek to enter in, and shall not be able. — Luke 13:24.

I am the Way.— John 14:6.

I am the Door.— John 10:7, 9.

By me if any man enter in, he shall be saved, and shall go in and out and find pasture. — John 10:9.

Enter ye in at the strait gate: for wide is the gate, and broad is the way, that leadeth to destruction, and many there be which go in thereat. Because strait is the gate, and narrow is the way which leadeth unto life, and few there be that find it. — Matt. 7:13, 14.

To him that overcometh will I grant to sit with me on my throne. Behold I have set before thee an open door, and no man can shut it. — Rev. 3:21, 8.

1 Ability to make the Heights, living to, and in, the New Age and overcoming death, is especially indicated by one's freedom from the thought of marriage and turning wholly from marrying or being given in marriage.

2 All expectancy of happiness through finding a mate on the earth must be turned to Christ, as the one spiritual Bridegroom, to God, as the one Husband. "Thy maker is thy husband," (Is. 54:5).

3 In the regeneration, every woman is to the candidate, his Mother or Sister, every man, her Father or Brother, and these relationships are with the Christ within each.

4 The union with the Universal is realized through giving the closest relationship, that human beings can have, to God, Christ and the Holy Spirit, finding the Bridegroom in these, likewise the Bride.

5 The portals of immortality are opened only to Virginity, which is first a consciousness, completed by the outer form of being sealed unto the Lord.

6 The heart and mind receive the seal when all one's generative powers are turned from flesh use and carnal pleasure. Then the psychical nature is sealed from astral imposition, as we read in Ezekiel 9:4 ("the mark," according to Tertullian was the Tau Cross) and Rev. 7:3. "Sealed in their foreheads" is more literally, in the top of the head, where we are psychically open, as a babe is physically open, until the Master of Regeneration has sealed us, as fruit is sealed with wax and so protected from the fermentation of corruption and death.

7 Then follows the sealing of the body as in a virgin state, so that the physical skin hermetically (so called because of the magic of Hermes or Thoth, god of thought) seals the whole body from the intrusion of death and decomposition. "And after my skin hath compassed this body, in my flesh I shall see God [immortality]," Job 19:26 — Young's Translation combined with A. V.

8 While one appears to be in a sensual world, in order not to be "of it" there must be a perpetual alertness not to be seduced by the false suggestions of one's own old nature or by false prophets who do not accept Jesus Christ.

9 For more candidates have fallen by the wayside, who were near to their goal, by a false attitude as to sex than by any other error. Theirs is the failure of David, who through the weakness of sex desire became "a man of blood," causing the death of Bathsheba's husband, and so he could not build the house of the Lord, that is, his immortal body on the earth.

10 Keep "oil for your lamps" by conserving your creative powers, increasing in knowledge and in other ways "laying up treasures in heaven"; so shall you be a "wise virgin," ready for the cosmic consciousness when it shall descend upon you.

11 "Gird up your loins" by refraining from loose speech and habits and ways respecting sexual matters, yet "quit you like men" who are virile and free and a law unto themselves.

12 By this fine culture, all the senses grow very refined, alert, delicate and sensitive, so that one hears instantly the gentle knock of the True Self (the Bridegroom) and opens the Door to him immediately.

13 All are being called to this Perfect Life, and he who hears the call should not hesitate to call others as he sees they will listen. But no one is to be pressed to walk all the Way, for only those can enter the path to remain who have the inner urge. All shall be taught of God (John 6:45) eventually, and step upon the great Way. We can invite them to live this life but only God in them can respond to, and accept, this invitation.

14 Those who are able to enter the virgin life and there abide, are divided into three classes, according to Jesus (Matt. 19:12) : (1)

Those who from birth have been able to control their sex desire; (2) Those who have continued in the virgin life because circumstances have compelled it. It is as though there had been a secret understanding with their guardian angels, that he or she should be kept from lawless or even lawful carnal intercourse, because the desire to go all the Way would be greater.

15 The third class are those who may have lost their virginity through earthly marriage, or through ignorant license, or through assault. But when they learn that, to go all the Way they must become as a little child, or youths and maidens whose virginity is inviolate, then their hearts are given to the pure Christ life, and God works with them to deliver them finally from all external temptation and carnal approach.

16 With all the zeal in you, seek to go into the Way by the Absolute Truth and perfect obedience to the Christ. Many are trying to enter into this complete bliss, but only those will succeed who co-operate absolutely with Jesus Christ.

17 For Jesus Christ is the only one who has walked all the Way to translation in the sight of men. Enoch walked with God and pleased God and so was translated, but he took his secret with him. Therefore Jesus is the Way to be translated.

18 But the Ascension is more than translation. Enoch and Elijah were translated into the heavenly realm, but they know not the Way to be translated back into the earthly realm, but this was what Jesus accomplished. "By me if any man enter in he shall be saved and go in and out. I am the Door."

19 The Gate and the Way are so narrow that only one can walk that Way, and only one can enter that Gate or Door. That one is the Christ and to enter that Gate and not be challenged by the Porter (the Cherubims, Gen. 3:24; "To him [the Christ] the porter openeth," John 10:3) we must be able to give the password, "I am the Christ."

20 All mortality is in the broad road that leads to death and destruction. Back and forth, round and round they wander, yet the straight and narrow road runs right through and across the broad way, as the straight line runs through the serpentine "S" in the dollar mark. And any moment the wanderer can enter the Way if he will,

"How far is it to Heaven? Not very far my friend ; A single, hearty step Will all your journey end."

21 All roads may lead to Rome but only one road leads to Heaven. Only the Absolute Truth, with no dualism in it, contains all the principles. Only one Master, Jesus Christ, he who walked all the Way and entered in at the Door can guide, all other Masters, Gurus, Prophets, Law-givers and Saviors have

left their disciples to wander alone finally to die, falling short of the mark. But Jesus Christ though invisible still walks with his followers, and will continue to do so to the end of time.

22 Bend your whole being with all zeal, prayer, devotion, faithfulness, fullness of love, to co-operate with Christ who has overcome the world, the flesh and the devil; and you will find yourself on the throne of Christ with all power in heaven and on earth, with death under foot and with the Hosts of Heaven and the inhabitants of the earth glorifying God, that he has given such power and honor to men.

IV

Whosoever will come after me, let him deny himself and take up his cross and follow me. — Mark 8:38.

And he that taketh not his cross, and followeth after me, is not worthy of me. — Matt. 10:38.

Whosoever shall seek to save his life shall lose it; and whosoever shall lose his life shall preserve it. — Luke 17:33.

For whosoever will save his life shall lose it- and whosoever will lose his life for my sake shall find it. — Matt. 16:25.

How can ye believe which receive honour one of another and seek not the honour that cometh from God only — John 5:44.

I receive not honour from men. — John 5:41.

I seek not mine own glory. — John 8:50.

I seek not mine own will. — John 5 :30.

I can of mine own self do nothing.— John 5 :30.

The son can do nothing of himself. — John 5:19.

I speak not of myself. — John 14:10.

He that speaketk of himself seeketh his own glory: but he that seeketh his glory that sent him, the same is true and no unrighteousness is in him. — John 7:18.

Be not ye called Rabbi: for one is your Master, even Christ; and all ye are brethren. Neither be ye called masters: for one is your Master, even Christ. — Matt. 23:8, 10.

Why callest thou me good? There is none good but one, that is, God.— Matt. 19:17.

When ye have done all those things which are commanded you, say, We are unprofitable servants: we have done that which was our duty to do. — Luke 17:1 0.

For thine is the kingdom, and the power, and the glory, for ever. Amen. — Matt. 6:13.

Put off . . . the old man which is corrupt . . . and be renewed in the spirit of your mind, and . . . put on the new man which after God is created in righteousness and true holiness. — Eph. 4:22, 23, 24.

Ye have put off the old man with his deeds, and have put on the new man which is renewed in knowledge after the image of him that created him. — Col. 3:9, 10.

1 The selfless life is the magical power to draw God and to be filled with one's Divinity.

2 The human I am must become utterly nothing to human sense while the divine I AM takes its place.

3 This is an accomplishment utterly impossible without the conscious co-operation of Jesus Christ, who brings it to pass by his God-knowledge and power.

4 Perpetual, silent prayer to the Father to remove and dissolve the human selfhood must be the ready weapon of him who would make the attainment.

5 To annul and neutralize the subtle assertion of the human self means alertness, watchfulness and unceasing communion with one's Divinity.

6 For the little I am merges so completely into the great I AM that ultimately all that is declared applies (to human sense) to both, and no sharp line of distinction can be drawn.

7 Previous to that conscious at-one-ment, the little I am must be thoroughly cleansed of all sense of separate selfhood, which expresses itself as vanity, self-conceit, egotism, self-praise and pride.

8 Close the lips when tempted to tell something to one's own credit, or that will draw forth the admiration of others.

9 And if unconsciously you have told that which brings a response of praise from others, silently repeat "Thine the glory," "Thine the glory," until all personal feeling of self-satisfaction has subsided and become still.

10 For we can do and be nothing of ourselves. All the intelligence we have is God shining through. All the beauty is God-presence. All the skill, bravery, strength, wit, talent, genius, are from the Christ-self, and nothing comes from our human self.

11 Watch that no comparisons rise in your thoughts and so begin to voice through your lips, between yourself and others, such as "I would never do that."

12 Ordinary boasting, the spiritual know how to avoid, but the subtle tributes to one's human position, name, ability, etc. — all, one must learn to

repudiate, and this silently, lest even this act draw forth further expressions to be overcome. And the silent reminder can be, "Thou only! Thou only!"

13 Pride of family passes away. Is not the Divine in all humanity our family? We have but one Father, but one Ancestor, God. Every form of pride is put under foot by the power of the Spirit

14 Arrogance may He crouching quite unknown to us. If so, then we draw crosses. We are misunderstood, snubbed, blamed unjustly, neglected, insulted. When these appear, instead of resenting them, secretly rejoice that, by your non-resistance, some secret error is being dissolved and passing away forever.

15 Embrace every cross. Do not run away from your problems. Walk up to them and make yourself one with them through prayer and conscious co-operation with Christ, your yoke-fellow.

16 Be skillful so as not to antagonize others with your goody-goodness. Let not your good make others feel evil.

17 Let not your unselfishness hide from you the common forms of selfishness that rise from our beliefs in what are "our rights" and what "is due us." Watch self-congratulation upon "getting the best" of another, also the resentment and "blues" when another gets an advantage over you.

18 Not "What is there in it for me?" but "How can I serve another?" Not "Where do I come in?" but "What can I do for you?"

19 It is not enough to be unselfish. Let us break down all indifference to the welfare of our fellow beings. Let us love as Christ loves. It is Christ in us that does that. Pray for it.

20 Are you afraid to lose an advantage, a pleasure, some measure of praise, something that is your very life? Can you lose anything in reality? If you think you can, then lose it this moment in Christ. Let it go. Loose it.

21 Loose from your mind every sense of loss and be free. Then you'll find the reality of what you prize abiding with you forever and taking form after form.

22 Be fearless before public opinion. Be rightly indifferent to what "they say," so long as you know you are being true to your principles.

23 When you discover yourself thinking how you can please the ear of man and call forth his praise, fly to your heavenly Father, seeking his pleasure, to be honored only by him. Herein lies a secret of enlarging one's faith and power to believe.

24 Be finished with titles and the desire to be a leader, or to excel others in anything. Let your desire to excel be only to please God and honor the Truth.

25 As we walk all the way we shed the old life, form, loves and ways as the old leaves of the live-oak fall to earth with the coming of the new growth. We know with Paul, "I live, yet not I — it is Christ that lives in me."
V

By this shall all men know that ye are my disciples, if ye have love one to another. — John 13:35.

A new commandment I give unto you. That ye love one another; as I have loved you, that ye also love one another. As the Father hath loved me, so have I loved you.— John 13:34-15:9.

Love your enemies, bless them that curse you, do good to them that hate you and pray for them which despite' fully use you and persecute you. — Matt. 5:44.

For if ye love them which love you, what thank have ye for sinners also love those that love them. — Luke 6   :32.

And if ye do good to them which do good to you what thank have ye for sinners also do even the same. — Luke 6:33.

And as ye would that men should do to you, do ye also to them likewise. — Luke 6:31.

Give to him that asketh thee, and from him that would borrow of thee turn not thou away. — Matt 5:42.

And if ye lend to them of whom ye hope to receive, what thank have ye for sinners also lend to sinners, to receive as much again. — Luke 6:34.

And unto him that smiteth thee on the one cheek offer also the other; and him that taketh away thy cloak forbid not to take thy coat also. — Luke 6:29.

And why beholdest thou the mote that is in thy brother's eye, but perceivest not the beam that is in thine own eye— Luke 6:41.

Either how canst thou say to thy brother, Brother, let me pull out the mote that is in thine eye, when thou beholdest not the beam that is in thine own eye? Thou hypocrite cast out first the beam that is in thine own eye, then shall thou see clearly to pall out the mote that is in thy brother's eye. — Luke 6:42.

Forgive and ye shall be forgiven. I say not unto thee. Until seven times: but until seventy times seven. — Luke 6:37, Matt. 18:22.

Father forgive them, they know not what they do. — Luke 23:34.

Judge not and ye shall not be judged: condemn not and ye shall not be condemned: forgive and ye shall be forgiven. — Luke 6:37.

For if ye forgive men their trespasses, your heavenly Father will also forgive you. So likewise will my heavenly Father do also unto you, if ye from your hearts forgive not every one his brother their trespasses. — Matt. 6:14, Matt. 18:35.

1 Loving is the one supreme sign that one is in the Way. Though one have a correct belief, a faith that works miracles, a morality unimpeachable, a name for greatest philanthropy, yet if Love is not complete the attainment will not be made.

2 This Love is a gift of God and it rests in us as the presence of our heavenly Father. By faith in it and prayer for it, this Love is uncovered and expresses itself to perfection.

3 It draws no line with anyone. It does not wait to find lovableness but with every enemy finds only a larger opportunity to love — not in theory but actual love from day to day until success comes — the enmity has gone forever.

4 For every unkind thought another is sending, radiate a genuinely approving thought For every malicious word spoken to one's face, or reported as having been said, give a good word back either silently or audibly. Feel these in your heart by the help of God.

5 Those who are hating you, take special steps to do something good to them or for them — do it so secretly that none shall know until everything secret shall be revealed.

6 If anyone is treating you unjustly, snubbing you or ignoring you, holding you in contempt, scandalizing you or in any way tormenting, take each act as a pressure upon you to exude more of the perfume of your soul.

7 It is easy to love those who are loving to us, we can whirl in a circle of contentment when no opposition comes into our lives. Progress comes when opposition presses us out of our smug contentment with mediocrity.

8 Those who are degenerating can do good to those who are good to them. But regeneration means doing good to those who know us not, who cannot

make any return even to the extent of expressing appreciation.

9 All things are from the Lord, and if there be any opposition take it as from the Lord and all sting will be gone — peace only reigns.

10 Remember that all belongs to all and in giving, you are but passing one's own along to him. In such giving there is no loss. Who gives to the Lord, gains.

11 It is written, Thou shalt lend to many, but borrow from none. Who lends to the Christ without thought of return shall be delivered from imposition.

12 Take from your mind and heart all opposition, resentment, resistance and revenge, and the Way will become smooth so that you will walk it as upon winged feet.

13 If you can draw into your life a lawsuit make nothing of it. Trust the Spirit to defend you and if judgment goes against you, let not a ripple disturb your peace. Rather, run out to meet the demand upon you by giving more than is demanded. All these things are finished in mind.

14 What is well done in mind may never — if, to the world, not desirable — take place outwardly. Abraham's perfect surrender of Isaac in heart prevented the surrender of Isaac's form.

15 The eye that renews its youth becomes innocent of faultfinding; the mind, that remains sane, harbors no criticism. We remove the motes from the eye of our brother by making nothing of them.

16 Our world is a mirror. Let us remove every belief in the reality of evil from our consciousness, and our world shall be free from evil, even as our thought.

17 To walk every step of the fair Way to the Ascension, every wrong done to us must be forgotten never to come into mind again.

18 Substituting for the false belief about self, the Truth about the real Self of another, which is incapable of wronging anyone, is the forgiveness that heals.

19 Lift up your eyes from every untrue appearance, and fill them with the Christ-view, so shall your eyes be to the shadows of wrong as the sun to darkness.

20 Forgive forever and to the uttermost. Let no thought place limitation upon your forgiving power.

21 Let your forgiveness be more than a sentiment; see it as Power, the dynamo that dispels the darkness by replacing it with the light of Truth.

22 Who judges not according to appearance, judges not at all. For appearances are the combination of good and evil. Seeing no evil we have nothing to judge.

23 Condemnation is death — a mental stoning that in the end slays the slayer, therefore in the Way of Life there is no condemnation, because in the Way of Life there is no death.

VI

No man can serve two masters: for either he will hate the one, and love the other; or else he will hold to the one, and despise the other. Ye cannot serve God and mammon. —Matt. 6:24.

Take heed and beware of covetousness: for a man's life consisteth not in the abundance of the things which he possesseth. — Luke 12:15.

And he sent them to preach the kingdom of God, and to heal the sick. And he said unto them. Take nothing for your journey, neither staves, nor scrip, neither bread, neither money; neither have two coats apiece. — Luke 9 :23.

Thus said Jesus unto his disciples. Verily I say unto you. That a rich man shall hardly enter into the kingdom of God. And again I say unto you. It is easier for a camel to go through the eye of a needle than for a rich man to enter into the kingdom of God. — Matt. 19:23, 24.

So is he that layeth up treasure for himself and is not rich toward God. — Luke 12:21.

Jesus said unto him. If thou wilt be perfect, go and tell that thou hast, and give to the poor, and thou shalt have treasure in heaven; and come and follow me. — Matt. 19:21.

Sell that ye have, and give alms; provide yourselves bags which wax not old, a treasure in the heavens that failetk not.— Luke 12:33.

And why call ye me. Lord, Lord, and do not the things which I say? Whosoever cometh to me and heareth my sayings and doeth them, I will show you to whom he is like:

He is like a man which built an house, and digged deep, and laid the foundation on a rock: and when the flood arose, the stream beat vehemently upon that house, and could not shake it: for it was founded upon a rock.

But he that heareth, and doeth not, is like a man that without a foundation built an house upon the earth; against which the stream did beat vehemently, and immediately it fell; and the ruin of that house was great. — Luke 6:46-49.

For ye know the grace of our Lord Jesus Christ, that though he was rich yet for your sakes he became poor, that ye through his poverty might be rick. — 2 Cor. 8:9.

I have given you an example, that ye should do as I have done to you. — John 13:15.

Who then is a faithful and wise servant, whom his lord hath made ruler over his household, to give them meat in due season?

Blessed is that servant, whom his lord when he Cometh shall find so doing.

Verily I say unto you. That he shall make him ruler over all his goods. — Matt. 24:45-48.

1 The love of money cannot exist in the heart of the devotee who desires to love God and humanity with his whole heart.

2 Therefore do nothing for the sake of money. Give no respect or consideration to it; nor let it, or the lack of it, be the reason for any of your movements or of your stillness.

3 God is the only Power; all the power that money seems to have is what man gives it, and is but a reflected or secondary power. Acknowledge God as the only Reason and Power in all your ways.

4 Early you must decide whether you shall be influenced by money or by God; and all the Way, the consideration of money must be put into the background and under foot.

5 He who would run, or progress rapidly, in the Way of the Christ must know how to slip his wealth into the perpetual use and benefit of humanity.

6 So shall a man's stewardship remain, and he himself mount to the Highest.

7 All desire for possessions is transmuted to one supreme Desire for God.

8 Neither the loss nor the gain of things disturbs or excites the one who abides in Christ, for his peace and joy remaineth in him.

9 All our circumstances and associates are tools in God's hands, training us to be indifferent to worldly riches and independent of them.

10 Miraculous provision is one of the delights of the Way.

11 Accumulations of wealth act as the dust and stone under which to bury the bodies of their owners.

12 The shame of dying rich is the final fruit of the pride of living rich.

13 He who walks the Way must acquire the skill of the Christ, to distribute all that comes to him to his neighbors who have need, giving not only one-tenth but all that he has, and yet remain independent himself.

14 Trust-in-riches is secretly and faithfully transmuted in the heart of the Christ candidate to trust-in-God.

15 The "bags that wax not old" and the "house founded upon the rock" is the Body, immortal and efficient, that develops for the candidate who gives all for all and, not only listens to the Christ directions, but also practices them.

16 In the Way of the Christ, is also the highway of prosperity for it is the Path of Wisdom, in "whose right hand is length of days and in whose left hand are riches and honour."

17 The glorious insignia of God's prosperity are the enrichment, comfort and freedom that it brings to others beside the Candidate, through his service and knowledge of Truth.

18 To be rich and yet to appear to be in moderate circumstances, that others may be comfortable, is to walk with Jesus Christ who laid his own wealth on the altar that all might be rich.

19 The servant or steward who is "faithful to give his household, meat in due season" begins the distribution in consciousness, giving in mind first and then outwardly.

20 Give to the Christ in every one, those who seem unworthy as well as the worthy. There is only One to give to in every one, the Christ.

21 The generous giver wisely withholds until the first gift is made — the true thought:

"You are not poor; you are not a beggar; you are not deceiving ; you are not worthless. You are God's Beloved, you are the Christ."

22 The Inner Voice counsels whether to give or to withhold. Be not impulsive, be inspired.

23 It is Christmas day every day, when Christ is the giver and Christ the receiver of your bounty.

24 Be unselfish to the point of selflessness that does not even think of being unselfish.

25 Give in secret and in the open, in season and out of season, regardless of appreciation, gratitude or thanks.

26 And as graciously receive as you give. Bring all things to equity and equality; and know only kings to whom you give and, in turn receive, as kings from kings.

VII

I am come to send fire on the earth. — Luke 12:49.

For every one shall be tailed with fire. — Mark 9 :49.

Receive ye the Holy Ghost: whose soever sins ye remit, they are remitted unto them; and whose soever sins ye retain, they are retained. — John 20:22, 23.

Judge not and ye shall not be judged: condemn not and ye shall not be condemned; forgive, and ye shall be forgiven. — Luke 6:37.

But I say unto you. All sins will be forgiven the sons of men and evil speaking. But one, speaking evil against the Holy Spirit, may not be forgiven to the end of the age. but is liable to age-lasting judgment. — Literal Translation of Mark 3:28, 29.

Because they said. He hath an unclean spirit. — Mark 3:30.

I judge no man. — John 8:15.

For with what judgment ye judge, ye shall be judged. Matt. 7:2.

Verily, verily, I say unto you, He that heareth my word, and believeth on him that sent me hath everlasting life and shall not come into judgment, but is Passed from death unto life.— John 5 -24.

Howbeit when he, the Spirit of truth, is come, he will guide you into all truth . . . he dwelleth with you and shall be in you. — John 16:13 and 14:17.

The Comforter, which is the Holy Ghost, whom the Father will send in my name, he shall teach you all things. —John 14:26.

Ye shall be baptized with the Holy Ghost not many days hence. — Acts 1 :5.

1 In every Candidate for the Ascension there breaks forth the Fire of the Holy Spirit.

2 This Fire is sweet, and a delight to those who will not condemn others nor even judge them.

3 But this same Fire is hell to those who have not learned to refrain from criticizing and judging others, for they come under their own condemnation as well as suffering from the judgment dealt to them by others.

4 Receive this Holy Breath by forgiving to the uttermost and training your whole being to see no evil, hear no evil and speak no evil.

5 By utterly refusing to recognize evil in others you will escape the chief error of calling the Holy Spirit in another, an evil thing.

6 Only the Holy Spirit can teach us the Way to be loosened from our subtlest errors, and to accept the Truth, which we have continually rejected.

7 For as Master Builders we shall find that the rejected Stone, or Truth, becomes the Head of the corner, the finishing of our immortal body.

8 As long as evil is recognized in others, the Holy Breath may seem to leave us for a while — coming and going, as with the early Disciples and even Jesus before Ascension Day.

9 The Holy Spirit must be a permanent Presence to the senses of the Candidate who would escape all suffering and death on the Way to the Ascension Mount.

10 Jesus finished all suffering and death for every one who will understand his teaching, and will believe into his own Godhood here and now. Such have passed already from death to Immortality.

11 For only the Holy Spirit can guide one past the dangerous places where others have fallen.

12 And to hear the slightest whisper of the Inner Voice at any moment that its counsel is needed, the imagination and the hearing must be perfectly defended from evil reports.

13 Ceaseless prayer must be made for the consciousness of hearing the Voice of the Holy Spirit — daily declaration of its speaking within — until your ears are forever opened.

14 Then when the Voice of gentle silence has reached your inner ear, it itself will guide you to listen to it daily.

15 For there must be (1) no uncertainty about it; (2) it must be divinely impersonal; (3) one with the great impersonal Jesus Christ; and (4) wholly without interference from our intellect, feelings or senses.

16 All that Jesus Christ taught about the Inner Voice proves true in the experience of the devotee.

17 Study the Master's words about the Spirit of Truth, called the Comforter, also the Holy Spirit and the Holy Ghost in John, chapters 14, 15 and 16.

18 The Holy Spirit is within you now and is evermore speaking to you as "impressions," conscience, "that something," intuition, etc.

19 The Fire will reveal the work of the Holy Spirit in your life from the day of your first breath to the present moment. Its works last forever.

20 The Holy Breath and the Love Fire open your interior senses of seeing and hearing and your prophetic sense.

21 Waiting for the Holy Spirit to develop these, saves the devotee visions and experiences that are undesirable. "Wait on the Lord and he will bring it to pass."

22 To the life of sincere, faithful devotion come all the revelations, inspirations and other delights of the heavenly realm.

23 Though these gifts may seem long in manifestation, never be impatient nor disappointed. In all ways live, speak, act as though they were present now, for they are. Thereby shall you be ever ready, and never be taken unawares.

VIII

And he spake a parable unto them to this end, that men ought always to pray, and not to faint. — Luke 18:1.

And he said unto them. Which of you shall have a friend, and shall go unto him at midnight, and say unto him. Friend, lend me three haves. . . .

I say unto you, Though he will not rise and give him, because he is his friend, yet because of his importunity he will rise and give him as many as he needeth. — Luke 11:5-8.

And I say unto you Ask, and it shall be given you; seek, and ye shall find; knock, and it shall be opened unto you. — Luke 11:9,

If ye then, being evil, know how to give good gifts unto your children: how much more shall your heavenly Father give the Holy Spirit to them that ask him. — Luke 11:13.

And it came to pass, that, as he was praying in a certain place, when he ceased, one of his disciples said unto him, Lord, teach us to pray, as John also taught his disciples. —Luke 11:1.

And when thou prayest, thou shall not be as the hypocrites are . . . after this manner therefore pray ye. —Matt. 6:5-9.

And when ye stand praying, forgive, if ye have ought against any: that your Father also which is in heaven may forgive you your trespasses. — Mark 11:25,

All things whatsoever ye shall ask in prayer, believing, ye shall receive.— Matt. 21:21.

If ye shall ask anything in my name, I will do it. — John 14:14.

Watch ye therefore and pray always, that ye may be accounted worthy to escape all these things that shall come to pass, and to stand before the Son of man. — Luke 21:36.

1 The path direct to God is every step a prayer.

2 Therefore the successful follower of Christ learns to pray without ceasing.

3 Every temptation to fail, he makes an occasion to commune with God upon success.

4 Every suggestion to be sick, to be afraid, to be discouraged, to sin, to let go of life or any good, means to him more determination to talk with his , heavenly Father about Health, Faith, Courage, Love, Life and Good of every kind.

5 He will not be refused. He will never let go. He is the importunity that is irresistible.

6 Three loaves we must have for our Friend, our Divinity when it comes, perfection of body, mind and soul — God only can give us this Perfection.

7 Ask, seek, knock, day after day and believe into this Perfect Triune Man.

8 In its simplicity the fulfillment of every prayer is the receiving of the Holy Spirit of anything one may ask for.

9 Pray to know how to pray.

10 Ask the Holy Spirit to pray in you.

11 Do not pray the way that those do who receive no answers.

12 Change your own way of praying until realization conies; then you can repeat and repeat and it will not be vain, but effectual.

13 If doubt or discouragement begin to confuse or weaken you, then repeat the Lord's Prayer even though it be mechanical.

14 If your prayer is aloud, do not think how it sounds to human ears. Be silent before such thoughts.

15 A steady, faithful silence directed earnestly to God; a breathing, "Father!"; a fervent sentence "Thou knowest"; a stillness of "I believe," resting and waiting in the Presence — these are better than loud cries of feverish unbelief.

16 Study all that Jesus Christ has taught on prayer. Learn his words. Sink into his being, and pray to the Father as Jesus Christ's own self.

17 Above all things, remove all barriers of unforgiveness between yourself and your fellow beings; put away all criticism, all condemnation.

18 Realize you cannot ask for anything that has not already been given you. Prayer wipes out time and space between you and the receiving.

19 One hearty prayer full of faith and realization should be our first expression with expectancy of immediate answer.

20 If the response is not at once, then prayer should be continued not only in words but in new deeds, new thoughts, new feelings and new works of the Christ.

21 To have a body that can bear the new life, a mind strong before the new thoughts, a soul that will stand firm before its Divinity, and that one may escape all the disasters and calamities of the closing age, the Christian must be alert, and so prayer-filled, that he is the very Word itself, by which all things were and are made.

IX

I am the door; he that entereth in by the door is the shepherd of the sheep. To him the porter openeth. — John 10:7, 2, 3.

I am the door: by me if any man enter in he shall be saved and shall go in and out and find pasture. — John 10:9.

I am the living bread which came down from heaven: if any man eat of this bread, he shall live forever. — John 6:51.

My Father giveth you the true bread from heaven. I am the bread of life: he that cometh to me shall never hunger; and he that believeth on me shall never thirst. — John 6:32,35.

Abide in me and I in you. — John 15:4.

He that abideth in me and I in him, the same bringeth forth muck fruit; for without me ye can do nothing. — John 15:5.

If ye abide in me and my words abide in you, ye shall ask what ye will, and it shall be done unto you. — John 15:7.

That they all may be one; as thou. Father, art in me, and I in thee, that they also may be one in us. — John 17:21.

He that hath seen me hath seen the Father. I and the Father are one.— John 14:9 and 10:30.

Know ye not your own selves, how that Jesus Christ is in you.—2 Cor. 13:5.

For as many of you as have been baptized into Christ have put on Christ.— Gal. 3 :27.

Put ye on the Lord Jesus Christ— Rom. 13:14.

The mystery which hath been hid from ages . . . which is Christ in you. — Col. 1:26, 27.

Christ is all, and in all.— Col. 3:11.

That we may present every man perfect in Christ Jesus: for in him dwelleth all the fullness of the Godhead bodily and ye are complete in him. — Col. 1:28 and 2:9,10.

I live; yet not I but Christ liveth in me: and the life which I now live in the flesh, I live by the faith of the Son of God.— Gal. 2:20.

1 Man is one being, not a million. And as One Being only can he attain immortality in the flesh and the Ascension.

2 Jesus Christ demonstrated his identity with God and with Man, therefore his is the mind and the heart that thinks and feels truly.

3 Man is making the same achievement, thinks the same thoughts and feels the same feelings.

4 Therefore to cross the portals of Eden, or go through the Door of the Ascension, Man must go as Jesus Christ.

5 The name Jesus Christ is the password; to him that says, "I am Jesus Christ," the sentinel says, "He knows, let him pass."

6 But if he has not the "wedding garment," (Matt. 22:11, 12) the body prepared for the heavenly consciousness, he cannot remain, but is presently back in the ordinary thinking.

7 And none can have the immortal body except those who are fed on, and nourished by, the Truth, the substance and the life ("flesh and blood") of Jesus Christ.

8 We eat this Bread from Heaven by thinking Christ's thoughts, meditating upon his words, making them our very own, and living his life.

9 As baby bees become queen bees through being fed upon royal bee-bread, so those that eat Christ become Christ in the flesh.

10 In truth, we are already Christ. The appearance of becoming Christ is only in the flesh, the realm of demonstration.

1 God and Christ are the same. Jesus proved this, and the one who merges himself into Jesus Christ will prove the same truth.

12 Making the union with Jesus Christ is the beginning of unity with all humanity, whereby each is brought to his Father's house, fruits of the heavenly vine.

13 No other Master ever rose to the heights that Jesus achieved, therefore there is none can instruct us in that Way but Jesus. Other Masters may carry us far, but we abandon them for Christ when we aspire to our Godhood while yet in the flesh.

14 All things are possible to the Christ consciousness, and all that such devotees may wish comes to pass while they put their wish into the form of prayer.

15 Only God in you can reveal the truth that you are Christ

16 There is but one God and there is but one Man and he is the God-man, the reality of every human form.

17 Eat and drink the words of Jesus Christ, that have been passed down to us through inspirational memory, and as a special gift of God to his beloved world.

18 He who meditates upon Jesus' words, turning them over and over in mind; using them as his own; studying to get to the essence or spirit of them, will receive new thoughts every day, revelations and inspirations of untold value, making a life of infinite satisfaction.

glorify God by bringing forth fruits of healing of yourself and others, of sinless living, of peace, prosperity, and happiness for all through your silent, immutable decrees.

You are God's Living Decree of Good to this world. Let your light shine. " Thou shall decree," See this as a commandment, as imperative as any one of the Decalogue.

And God said, Let them have dominion over the earth. The hour cometh, and now is, when divine man, he that overcomes, takes to himself his mighty prerogatives, and whatever he wishes he brings to pass by pronouncing the magical words

"It is!"